CITYSPOTS
DUBL

Pat Levy

Written by Pat Levy
Updated by Margaret Thomas

Published by Thomas Cook Publishing
A division of Thomas Cook Tour Operations Limited
Company registration No: 1450464 England
The Thomas Cook Business Park, 9 Coningsby Road
Peterborough PE3 8SB, United Kingdom
Email: books@thomascook.com, Tel: +44 (0)1733 416477
www.thomascookpublishing.com

Produced by The Content Works Ltd
Aston Court, Kingsmead Business Park, Frederick Place
High Wycombe, Bucks HP11 1LA
www.thecontentworks.com

Series design based on an original concept by Studio 183 Limited

ISBN: 978-1-84157-984-9

First edition © 2006 Thomas Cook Publishing
This second edition © 2008 Thomas Cook Publishing
Text © Thomas Cook Publishing
Maps © Thomas Cook Publishing/PCGraphics (UK) Limited
Republic of Ireland maps: reproduced from Ordnance Survey Ireland Permit No. 8494
© Ordnance Survey Ireland and Government of Ireland
Transport map © Communicarta Limited

Project Editor: Linda Bass
Production/DTP: Steven Collins

Printed and bound in Spain by GraphyCems

Cover photography (O'Connell Street and Liffey River bridge)
© Dallas & John Heaton/Alamy

CONTENTS

SYMBOLS KEY

The following symbols are used throughout this book:

ⓐ address ☎ telephone ⓦ website address ⓔ email
🕒 opening times Ⓝ public transport connections ❶ important

The following symbols are used on the maps:

🅸	information office	▨	points of interest
✈	airport	O	city
✚	hospital	O	large town
🛡	police station	○	small town
🚍	bus station	═	motorway
🚆	railway station	━	main road
✝	cathedral	─	minor road
❶	numbers denote featured cafés & restaurants	—	railway

Hotels and restaurants are graded by approximate price as follows:
£ budget price ££ mid-range price £££ expensive

The following abbreviations are used in the addresses:

Av.	Avenue
Rd	Road
St	Street

◗ *Take a walk over the famous Ha'penny Bridge*

INTRODUCING
Dublin

Introduction

Dublin is a curious mix of ancient and modern. On the one hand the city celebrates its Viking past and on the other erects gorgeous low-rise, ecologically sound, high-tech buildings on vast tracts of old warehouses that have lain derelict for generations. It rejoices in its membership of the EU and its role in peace-keeping but remembers the 200 or so martyrs of the doomed-to-fail 1916 Uprising; it consults with its nearest neighbour, Britain, on matters of importance but go into any pub when there's a football match between England and any other country in the world, and see whose side Dubliners are on.

Dublin is a great place to visit. It has its tourist infrastructure so polished you can see your face in it, hotels are on-line, wireless, hip places, or, if you prefer, quaint, 'olde worlde', loaded with antiques and full of ethnic charm. People come here for the craic (Irish fun); Dubliners really know how to enjoy themselves, and they exercise that talent at every opportunity. Dublin's bars and clubs heave with punters at weekends, big names perform at the Point and other venues, there are festivals coming out of the woodwork, culture in the form of classic theatre and opera, classical music hits you at every turn and there are more museums than you can shake a guidebook at. If all that sounds exhausting, the countryside is a 30-minute ride away on the DART rail system. Spend a day in the Wicklow mountains or stride the bracing cliff walk at Howth.

And food! No longer the gravy dinner, meat and two veg capital of the world, Dublin can offer you every cuisine imaginable, nipped and tucked to suit both the Irish palate and the diversity of the wallet content of its visitors. And the glory of the city is its size; tiny by the standards of any British city, all the places you really want to see are within walking distance of your hotel. Besides a guarantee of perfect weather (which they're working on, if they haven't sorted it out yet), can you ask for anything more?

◐ *Dublin city centre is always bustling with life*

When to go

Every time of the year is a good time to visit Dublin, though if you're coming armed with your new camera, it's in summer that the city looks at its best – blossom on the trees, the parks resembling the pictures on jigsaw boxes, the boat rides working, museums all open and lots and lots of open-air events.

SEASONS & CLIMATE

Weather-wise there's no telling when is the perfect time to visit Dublin. Its weather is notoriously changeable and you are just as likely to get two weeks of drizzle in the middle of August as blazing sunshine and bright sunny January days rather than grey, overcast ones. But, generally speaking, temperatures are quite mild all year, with very few days below zero, even in February. Summer temperatures average between 15 and 20°C (59 and 68°F), although the occasional scorcher of 26°C (79°F) or more has been known. Winter temperatures range between 5 and 10°C (41 and 50°F), with the odd few days of traffic chaos, flight delays and crunchy pavements while they remember where they left the gritting lorries.

ANNUAL EVENTS

January
Temple Bar Festival of Irish Culture (26–29 Jan) Lots of jigging and lots of fiddling at this celebration of the country's warm and rich culture. Ⓦ www.templebartrad.com

March
St Patrick's Day (15–19 Mar) Celebrations include a parade, green beer, music in the pubs and late-opening bars. Ⓦ www.stpatricksfestival.ie

May

International Gay Dublin Theatre Festival (First week May) The smell of the greasepaint, the roar of the crowd and the glitter of the sequins.
Ⓦ www.gaytheatre.ie

June

Diversions (June–Sept) A summer-long series of events based in the city, and especially in Temple Bar, ranging from free talks, musical performances and exhibitions to activities in the parks for children.

◉ *Sean Tyrell at the Temple Bar Festival of Irish Culture*

⬤ *The St Patrick's Day Festival is the most colourful event in Dublin*

Flora Women's Mini Marathon (First weekend June) Running a marathon is impressive; running one in heels is awesome. Ⓦ www.womensminimarathon.ie

Dublin Writer's Festival (Mid-June) A gathering of some super-heavyweight literary names. Ⓦ www.dublinwritersfestival.com

Bloomsday (16 June) A celebration of the book that many buy and few ever read (see page 12).

August
Dublin Gay and Lesbian Film Festival (First weekend Aug) A fabulosa fest of pink-tinged pics. Ⓦ www.gaze.ie

The Liffey Swim (Late Aug) In which 400 or more contestants swim 2.5 km (1 ½ miles) from Rory O'More Bridge to Custom House Quay.

September
GAA All-Ireland Senior Hurling Final This is what you call a sport and, boy, do they go for it! Ⓦ www.gaa.ie

October
Dublin City Marathon (Late Oct) Fun-runners, top athletes and those fuelled by Guinness and self-belief lace up and let rip.
Ⓦ http://adidasdublinmarathon.ie

PUBLIC HOLIDAYS
New Year's Day 1 Jan
St Patrick's Day 17 Mar
Easter Monday 13 Apr 2009; 5 Apr 2010
May Holiday First Mon in May
June Holiday First Mon in June
August Holiday First Mon in Aug
October Holiday Last Mon in Oct
Christmas Day 25 Dec
St Stephen's Day 26 Dec

On public holidays lots of shops close or have shorter hours, banks close and sights either close or operate with Sunday opening hours. Check each sight before you visit. Pubs close altogether on Good Friday (not a public holiday) and Christmas Day.

Bloomsday

Bloomsday celebrates one of the most important, and probably least read, novels of the 20th century. In *Ulysses*, James Joyce writes about the peregrinations of an advertising salesman around the city of Dublin on 16 June 1904. He is the Jew, Leopold Bloom, an outsider and wanderer like Ulysses, and each of the chapters of the novel corresponds to an event from Homer's *Odyssey*. As he wrote the book, Joyce (living in exile in Europe – 'Ireland is the old sow that eats her farrow', his alter ego Stephen Dedalus says) carefully reconstructed the streets and buildings of the city, writing home to family and friends to check that Bloom's footsteps were perfect. Over the last decade or so, the small numbers of intellectuals celebrating the novel informally on 16 June has swelled to hundreds. The day now involves, besides the talks and tours and guest speakers, hundreds of people dressed up in Edwardian costumes at each of the major sites of events in the novel and at the times that Bloom was fictionally there. If you have never read the novel, no matter – very few people taking part have. The people at each site will tell you the story and you can join one of the groups following sections of Bloom's walk (the entire novel would be exhausting). The chemist shop, Swenys, sells out of lemon-scented soap (Bloom buys the soap there for his bath in the public bath house), Davy Byrne's, 'the moral pub', sells tonnes of gorgonzola cheese and burgundy (Bloom's lunch) and Stephen Dedalus lives again in the Martello Tower in Sandycove. Check the website (🅦 www.jamesjoyce.ie) to see which sites are being focused on when you visit, but look out for events at Eccles Street (Bloom's home), Brown Thomas in Grafton Street (see page 68), Davy Byrne's in Duke Street (see page 72), College Green (see page 65), Temple Bar (see page 74) and the Martello Tower in Sandycove (see page 130).

The irony of it all is that *Ulysses* was banned in Ireland for decades, long after other countries had recognised its value as literature. Better late than never.

⬤ *James Joyce: one of the most famous writers of the 20th century*

History

Things went well in Ireland for a long time; the Stone Age, St Patrick, Christianity... all progress of a kind. During Europe's Dark Ages, the 6th, 7th and 8th centuries, Ireland was a beacon of humanity and learning, with its own laws, customs and schools, and Dublin was a settlement among many others with a mixture of Vikings and Gaels living in relative harmony. Dublin got bigger and minted its own coins. In the 12th century, the English turned up, killed a bunch of people, bullied their way into the city, and then, like the Vikings before them, succumbed to the persuasive charms of the Irish, inter-married, took up speaking Gaelic, and all was well – for a time.

In 1536 Henry VIII needed some extra cash and wanted a new wife so he disestablished the Church of England, closed all the Irish monasteries and started the real trouble. In 1607 many of the leading noblemen fled from Ireland, unwilling to take up the new religion and rule. Dublin became a military town, its Catholic majority ruled by a few heavily armed Protestants. Dublin prospered, grew, had beautiful buildings built under British rule, but no one was very happy about it. In 1690 James II attempted to take Ireland back from the Protestant William of Orange and his defeat led to the penal laws against Catholics. The Catholic Irish majority of the city were denied the right to own land, practise their religion and, later, vote.

The centuries since that time are marked in Dublin's history as a series of failed rebellions against the British. In 1798 the United Irishmen were based in the city and were defeated by government troops. In 1803 a spectacularly unsuccessful coup took place in Dublin led by Robert Emmet. In 1829 things improved slightly when Daniel O'Connell, a Catholic, was voted into the British Parliament and the last of the penal laws against Catholics was repealed. In

1845–49 Dublin was filled with thousands of desperate, starving people searching for food as the potato crop repeatedly failed for four years. The year 1867 saw further loss of life as the Irish Republican Brotherhood tried their hand at getting rid of the British. In 1870 land reform allowed Irish tenant farmers to buy their land, but not their freedom from British rule. Then in 1916 about 2,000 dedicated, idealistic men and women tried to take the city, stir the population to arms and send the British packing. It didn't work. The leaders were executed and people have been dying with photographs of the martyrs in their pockets ever since.

The year 1921 saw the signing of the Anglo-Irish Treaty and the resulting, less-than-successful independence of Southern Ireland. Rather unfortunately, the Irish took to fighting each other for a couple of years and then settled down to enjoy their freedom by banning everything from contraception to *Ulysses*. Seventy years or so of economic depression, emigration and having to travel backwards and forwards to Britain for abortions and condoms followed, and then the Celtic Tiger was born, transforming the Irish economy.

In the last decade of the 20th century, Dublin – so often thought of as a poor relation in the family of European capitals – suddenly blossomed into a seriously cool place. This was largely due to a rash of popular culture giants such as U2, Boyzone and Roddy Doyle, whose mass-media friendliness and resulting influence raised the city's profile. As a consequence, investment poured in, hotels, galleries and museums sprang up and Dublin took off. Now, with the Republic of Ireland having Europe's most buoyant economy, its number-one city is established as a 21st-century superstar destination.

Lifestyle

Dublin is a modern, forward-looking, European city, its workforce one of the youngest and most well-educated in Europe. With a huge student population and thousands of young Eastern Europeans willing to take up unskilled work, it is no wonder that there is so much for young people to do, and so many opportunities to spend hard-earned money in the city. The city's weekends are for the young; after midnight the central streets belong to the party-goers and it is possible to spend the entire weekend without sobering up if only you know the right places to go. Dublin's young don't remember when condoms were a political issue or a green card was a means of getting some prospects. Some form unions not sanctioned by the church, become single parents, adopt lifestyles that their parents never dreamed of, own their own flats in regenerated parts of the city, plan to buy a second home in the Irish countryside, and go to church only for weddings and funerals and special occasions or perhaps don't go at all.

Dublin is a family city too. Outside the city centre with its clubs and shops, life in the suburbs is a quieter, slower business. Many families still observe the old ways of life – three or more children, church on Sundays, or even daily, family dinners in the evening while watching Coronation Street or one of the Sky channels, the extended family close by. They sigh over the many tribunals investigating all sorts of corruption, tut over the number of foreigners in their city (although many of them would come to the defence of anyone being abused) and plan their holidays somewhere warm away from the Dublin weather.

Lots of Dubliners are newcomers, people who have moved to the city from small Irish towns or from further afield, Europe, the

US or Africa. For the first time, Dublin has a sizeable population of non-Christians of all kinds, lapsed or otherwise; more people speak Chinese in the city than Gaelic; and all shades of colour can be seen making a life in what was for centuries a Christian, conservative monoculture.

◆ *Trinity College attracts many national and international students*

Culture

Even if the most popular form of culture in Dublin is found at the bottom of a pint glass, there are other forms of culture alive and kicking in the city. Dublin has a strong, if conservative, theatre tradition, a huge live music repertoire from classical and operatic to traditional bands, jazz and rock, a strong dance tradition covering classical ballet, Riverdance clones and modern dance and salsa classes. Its art galleries are remarkable for such a small country and its museums are lively hands-on places, often providing the venue for free performances and recitals. Most of all, the streets and parks themselves are like galleries, with some stunning (and occasionally naff) street art to which Dubliners have affectionately given nicknames (see page 20).

Theatre buffs will enjoy Dublin's offerings. The theatre festival in September (see Ⓦ www.dublintheatrefestival.com for details), accompanied by a fringe festival, brings in theatre groups from around the world and every venue is booked for middle-of-the-road drama, experimental drama, and everything in between. But even outside festival time it is worth checking the listings magazines (see below) for theatrical happenings.

WHAT'S ON?

Listings for most cultural events and performances are to be found in the magazines *Event Guide* (also available on-line at Ⓦ www.eventguide.ie) and *In Dublin* (also available on-line at Ⓦ www.indublin.ie), which can be picked up for free from cafés, newsagents and hotels.

Classical music and opera is less obvious in the city but it thrives quietly. Here again, the listings are essential. The city has two orchestras, the National Symphony Orchestra and the RTÉ Concert Orchestra. Opera Ireland puts on a season of works every other year at the Gaiety Theatre (see page 72), and there are regular chamber

◯ *Taking Irish music to the streets*

STREET ART

Many of the city's pieces of street art have been given nicknames by Dubliners; 'the queer with the sneer' for the statue of Oscar Wilde in Merrion Square, 'the tart with the cart' for the Molly Malone statue, 'the hags with the bags' for a statue of two women chatting, 'the stiletto in the ghetto' for the tower of light, to name a few. In 1999 an enormous clock on a pole, counting down to the millennium, was inserted into the Liffey River. It became known as 'the time in the slime'. When it broke down and was removed, its name changed overnight to 'the gap in the crap'.

music concerts at the Project Arts Centre (see page 85), Christ Church Cathedral (see page 77), Dublin City Gallery The Hugh Lane (see page 90), and **St Stephen's Church** (❷ Mount St Upper ❶ (01) 288 0663).

Two modern dance troupes operate out of Dublin: the Irish Modern Dance Theatre and the Dance Theatre of Ireland. For performances by them and other visiting dance ensembles, consult the listings.

Many of the city's museums and galleries were purpose-built and begun in the 19th century. Art galleries have benefited from several donations to the state, including the collection from Russborough House (see page 134), Hugh Lane's collection of art, and the art collection of Chester Beatty.

❿ *Pedestrianised Grafton Street is a major shopping area*

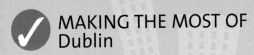

MAKING THE MOST OF
Dublin

Shopping

It's not the place you'd take a plane to in order to do your shopping, but Dublin has some good offerings for the consumer. The city has two major shopping areas; Grafton Street, where the Irish Institution, Brown Thomas (see page 68) and lots of British chain stores line the pedestrianised street, topped by the busy **St Stephen's Green Shopping Centre** (Ⓐ Grafton St Ⓦ www.stephensgreen.com), and O'Connell Street and its side roads where there are several British and Irish department stores, numerous shopping centres, a street market and lots of odd discount stores, especially along Earl Street North and Talbot Street.

Prices in the shops in Dublin fluctuate against prices in UK shopping centres. The chain stores often put the price in both sterling and euros on their goods, so you can see what you would be paying in England for the same item. The number of people in border towns such as Dundalk who make trips over the border into the north to do their shopping rather suggests, though, that there are better bargains to be had in Northern Ireland.

The things to look out for in Dublin are the many attractive, hand-made clothes and housewares, made in small workshops all over the country and for sale in shops such as the Kilkenny Store (see page 68) or other shops along Nassau Street, Leinster Street South and Dawson Street. Look out for hand-made and hand-woven tweed outfits, hand-knitted jumpers, beautiful, imaginative jewellery crafted in silver and other metals, pottery ranging from things to hold spent matchsticks to entire dinner services with matching cloths and lamps. Ironwork, too, has moved on from curly magazine holders to some beautiful minimalist lamps, tables, or sets of glass and wrought-iron drinking glasses.

Of course if it's something for the in-laws you're after, Dublin has that too – in bucket-loads. Felt leprechauns, tea towels with funny doggerel poems, giant green, gold and white hats with false hair sticking out, sets of Irish coffee glasses with the instructions printed on the side, shillelaghs... it's all still here.

🔺 *Inside St Stephen's Green Shopping Centre*

Eating & drinking

Dublin is awash with restaurants of all qualities and the scene has a high turnover rate: this year's place to be seen munching turns into next year's place to avoid at all costs, and the next thing you know it's a mobile phone shop.

You're best to look out for the places that offer traditional Irish cooking with a modern twist, where you'll be able to try dishes such as *champ* (mashed potatoes and scallions mixed with lots of butter), *boxty* (potato and flour pancakes), *colcannon* (cabbage and potato), or some of the traditional Irish breads such as soda farls, leavened with bicarbonate of soda instead of yeast. Ethnic cuisines also feature largely in what was once a meat and two veg city. There are excellent Mexican, Italian, Indian and Thai places all serving innovative dishes, even an inexpensive Nepalese place that has lasted for decades and can count celebs among its regular customers.

The restaurant's location is another factor to take into account when choosing where to eat. Temple Bar is the city's tourist ghetto and there are places there that would go out of business in a week if the tourists disappeared. There are, however, also some excellent, stylish, if possibly overpriced, places that justify giving your credit card an airing. The area north of St Stephen's Green has some long-established but, again, pricey places, while Dawson Street is home

PRICE CATEGORIES

Café and restaurant ratings in this book are based on the average price of a three-course dinner without drinks.

£ up to €20   ££ €20–45   £££ over €45

EATING & DRINKING

⬤ Temple Bar area has a wide choice of pubs and restaurants

to lots of café bars where you can eat, drink, chat and often listen to some live music. North of the river has always been a bit of a food desert but this, too, is improving with the new rejuvenated docks and IFSC area (see page 86) coming into their own.

Several of the city's restaurants have special menus, often called 'early bird', 'theatre' or just plain 'tourist' menus, which consist of a limited number of dishes from the evening à la carte available for an hour or two around 18.00–19.30 at reduced prices. If you want to eat early and not make a night of it, these can be a good option.

◔ *One of the pretty cafés on Dawson Street*

Finding a place for lunch is the least of your worries in the city. Most pubs make their profits from pub lunches and you are never more than a short walk from a pub in the city. The area around St Stephen's Green can become a bit fraught when the office workers come out for lunch, while the further out of the centre you travel the less imaginative the pub lunch.

In summer, eating outside is always an option, especially if you have children in tow or are on a budget. Parks such as St Stephen's Green (see page 64) or **Iveagh Gardens** (❷ behind Harcourt St) are open during daylight hours and are free, and along the river there are lots of spots to sit and munch while people-watching. There are good delicatessen shops in the city centre and all supermarkets have ready-made sandwiches.

A strict smoking ban operates in all public buildings in Ireland, including pubs and restaurants (and hotel rooms). Most pubs have managed to find a little space in the open, euphemistically called a beer garden but more likely where they used to store the beer barrels. These are heated in winter by environmentally unfriendly gas braziers and often have an awning, so the nicotine-challenged can keep out of the rain. Lots of cafés have found space on the street for a similar arrangement.

The dress code in bars and restaurants is relaxed to say the least. Some very upmarket restaurants may ask men to wear a jacket, while clubs have a dress code which the bouncers seem to make up as the night and the queues outside progress but which generally involves the not-wearing of trainers.

Vegetarians will have a hard time of it in the city. There are few dedicated vegetarian restaurants and while most places have a veggie option, it's pretty much a lip service affair. Indian restaurants of course are always a good option, and fish-eating non-meat eaters will find themselves well catered for.

Entertainment & nightlife

Sometimes it seems there are two Dublins. There is the day-time, working city where rules are properly followed, red lights are obeyed, and opening and closing hours are adhered to. Then there is Friday-night and weekend Dublin, when the streets are reclaimed by those lost boys and girls who would like to be free spirits but just enjoy the cash-flow created by working for a living. For the young and healthy of liver, Dublin rocks from office-closing hours on Friday to winding down in a club on Sunday. Visitors can tap into this alcohol-fuelled weekend life of the Dubliners, although in Temple Bar and the city centre most nights throughout the week are also pretty lively till the early hours.

For those who want to live on the wild side, it is necessary to leave the rather corny music of Temple Bar and venture out. Try a life-affirming pub crawl along South Great George's Street and swing suavely over to one of the clubs in Harcourt Street, Wexford Street or Leeson Street.

WHAT'S ON?

Good places to check out what's on are some of the music stores or pubs that serve food during the day. Papers such as the free *Event Guide*, the monthly *Slate* or the glossy *In Dublin*, will give a good idea of what's happening in a city where clubs go out of fashion as quickly as last year's platform soles. All are available free from cafés, newsagents and hotels.

● *The popular Temple Bar pub*

There are good places to hear live music of all descriptions in the city, from the stuff they churn out in Temple Bar for the tourists to some excellent small pubs which offer traditional musicians or good local rock music.

If it's a hooley you're looking for, there are several places which put on Irish traditional dance and music shows, a kind of amalgam of Riverdance and real Irish dancing. The **Arlington Hotel** in Bachelors Walk (☎ (01) 804 9100) has nightly music and dance shows.

Considering the number of comics Ireland has produced, the city has few really good stand-up venues, although a few places have

◆ *Experience the essence of the Irish here*

one or two nights dedicated to comedy. Again, check the listings since these places change frequently, but good places to seek out are the Ha'penny Bridge (see page 84), The International (see page 72) and The Sugar Club (see page 73).

There is the usual range of multi-screen theatres (see page 46), but also the **Irish Film Centre** (🄰 6 Eustace St 🄸 (01) 679 3477 🄦 www.filmcentre.co.uk), which shows independent, foreign and documentary films, and **Screen** (🄰 D'Olier St 🄸 0818 300 3301), which shows a mixture of arthouse and mainstream movies. Dublin absolutely loves a film festival, and in summer movies are shown in the open air at Meeting House Square (see page 76).

Sport & relaxation

SPECTATOR SPORTS

Football

Football in Dublin means one team and one team only: the almighty, all-conquering **Shamrock Rovers** (ⓦ www.shamrockrovers.ie), the secret of whose success is that they're the only half-decent outfit in the country. Long without a home ground, they hope one day to ply their silky skills at the Tallaght Stadium, just south of the city. Rumours of its being completed in 2009 or 2010 seem risibly optimistic.

International matches are traditionally played at Landsdowne Road (see opposite). Until its renovation is complete, they take place at Croke Park (see opposite).

Gaelic Football

Gaelic football is played by 15-strong teams who are allowed to handle the ball as well as kick it; it is probably closer to rugby than football. Amateur games are played at **Phoenix Park** (ⓔ Ashtown Gate, near Castleknock ⓣ (01) 677 0095) at weekends, but **Croke Park** is the main stadium (ⓔ Jones's Rd, Drumcondra ⓣ (01) 836 3222 ⓦ www.gaa.ie) for pro matches.

Greyhound racing

There are two main venues for watching gullible pooches belt around the track:

Harold's Cross Racetrack ⓔ 151 Harold's Cross Rd ⓣ (01) 479 1081 ⓛ 20.00 Mon, Tues & Fri. Admission charge

Shelbourne Park Stadium ⓔ Lotts Rd, Ringsend ⓣ (01) 668 3502 ⓛ 20.00 Wed, Thur & Sat. Admission charge

Horse racing

Leopardstown Racetrack (ⓐ Foxrock ⓣ (01) 289 0500
ⓦ www.leopardstown.com) is the place to for those who like a flutter
on the gee-gees. It has over 20 meetings a year, and Éireann operates
a special race-day bus service (call ⓣ (01) 873 4222 for details).

Rugby

Lansdowne Road Stadium (ⓐ 48 Mount St Lower) is the venue
for the domestic Leinster Senior Cup matches and the Six Nations
international games. However, the Stadium is closed until April 2010
and until then games are played at **Croke Park** (ⓐ Jones's Rd
ⓣ (01) 647 3800 ⓦ www.crokepark.ie).

PARTICIPATION SPORTS

Swimming

You can splash about to your heart's content at the magnificent
National Aquatic Centre (ⓐ Snugborough Rd, Blanchardstown
ⓣ (01) 646 4300 ⓦ www.nac.ie).

Tennis

There are tennis courts for hire in the following parks. If you've got the
balls, just turn up, pay and play: **Albert College Park** (ⓐ Glasnevin);
Bushy Park (ⓐ Terenure); **Herbert Park** (ⓐ Ballsbridge); **St Annes Park**
(ⓐ Raheny).

RELAXATION

Jogging

Phoenix Park (see page 103), **Iveagh Gardens** (ⓐ behind Harcourt St),
the Grand Canal towpaths, and Herbert Park in Ballsbridge, all make
good locations for jogging your way to a state of bliss.

Accommodation

Dublin has accommodation ranging from super exclusive boutique hotels to dorm beds in hostels and all of them are very much in demand in the high season or when a big event is on in the city, so it is best to book before you arrive. As the city becomes wealthier, more top-end hotels are appearing, and budget places upgrade to get the most out of the booming tourist trade. The most luxurious places are, generally speaking, south of the river around Merrion Square, St Stephen's Green and further out in Ballsbridge. The O'Connell Street area has the majority of budget hotels and guesthouse accommodation. Its advantage over Ballsbridge is its central location. Its disadvantage is that it can get noisy at night. Temple Bar has become a little enclave for party-going. It is possible to spend a weekend in Temple Bar and never leave. Its hotels are good 3-star quality, but like O'Connell Street, the area can be noisy at night.

HOTELS

Abbey Hotel £ Small, comfortable hotel with its own car park.
🄰 52 Abbey St Middle 🄱 (01) 872 8188 🄌 www.abbey-hotel.com
🄽 Bus: 16A to O'Connell St

Bewleys Hotel Ballsbridge £ Probably the best value in the city, a 3-star hotel with 1-star rates. Part of a small chain. Great restaurant, too.
🄰 Merrion Rd, Ballsbridge 🄱 (01) 668 1111 🄌 www.bewleyshotels.com
🄽 Aircoach

Jurys Croke Park Hotel £ Friendly hotel with a sporty theme. Everything you could ask for in a room, plus internet access. 🄰 Croke Park Stadium, Jones's Rd 🄱 (01) 871 4444 🄌 www.jurysdoyle.com/crokepark 🄽 Bus: Drumcondra Station

PRICE CATEGORIES
Ratings are based on the average price of a double room
per night in high season, including breakfast.
£ up to €90   **££** €90–200   **£££** over €200

Jurys Inn Christchurch £ Big, functional place which charges a room
rate – great if you have children. Good location, out of the hubbub
but close to the sights. ⓐ Christchurch Place ① (01) 454 0000
ⓦ www.jurysinns.com ⓝ Bus: 16A to Dame St

Jurys Inn Custom House £ Another branch of the good-value chain
of hotels. Room rate covers up to three adults or family of four.
ⓐ Custom House Quay ① (01) 607 5000 ⓦ www.jurysinns.com
ⓝ Bus: 748 to Terminus

Kelly's Hotel £ Small, family-owned and family-run hotel in a good
location for all the sights and nightlife. ⓐ 36 South Great George's St
① (01) 677 9277 ⓦ www.kellyshtl.com ⓝ Bus: 16A to Georges St

Phoenix Park House £ Small, family-run guesthouse close to
Phoenix Park. Bus ride into the city centre. Lots of facilities and
a good bargain. ⓐ 38–39 Parkgate St ① (01) 677 2870
ⓦ www.dublinguesthouse.com ⓝ Luas: Heuston Station

Best Western Academy Plaza Hotel £–££ Located in a quiet street off
O'Connell Street with all the facilities of a good 3-star hotel. Free Wi-Fi,
too. ⓐ Findlater Place ① (01) 878 0666 ⓦ www.academyplazahotel.ie
ⓝ Bus: 16A to O'Connell St

Best Western Ashling Hotel £–££ Small, busy place, a good way out of the city centre but close to a good bus route. ⓐ Parkgate St ⓣ (01) 677 2324 ⓦ www.bestwestern.ie ⓝ Luas: Heuston Station

Mespil Hotel £–££ Big, modern hotel on the bank of the Grand Canal, well out of the noise and bustle of Dublin's nightlife. ⓐ Mespil Rd ⓣ (01) 488 4600 ⓦ www.leehotels.com ⓝ Bus: 11 to Mespil Rd

Camden Court Hotel ££ Large, purpose-built hotel right in the heart of nightclub territory. Close enough to sights, and offering a pool and fitness centre. ⓐ Camden St ⓣ (01) 475 9666 ⓦ www.camdencourthotel.ie ⓝ Bus: 16A to Camden St

● *Enjoy a hearty breakfast at Egan's House Hotel*

Egan's House Hotel ££ Small, comfortable and friendly guesthouse in quiet, suburban location close to the Botanic Gardens. An excellent choice if all the palaver of the city gets you down. ⓐ 7 Iona Park, Glasnevin ⓣ (01) 830 3611 ⓦ www.eganshouse.com ⓝ Bus: 19 to Botanic Gardens

Leeson Inn ££ Slap-bang in the middle of everywhere that's worth going, the Leeson is strong on everything; a real plus are the business facilities for those who want to finish forging the data in that spreadsheet they should have completed before they came on holiday. ⓐ 26 Leeson St Lower ⓣ (01) 662 2002 ⓦ www.leesoninndowntown.com ⓝ Aircoach

The Morrison ££ A fashionable boutique hotel with the kind of luxurious atmosphere that makes you want to stay in and order room service. It has a spa and an excellent restaurant. ⓐ Ormond Quay Lower ⓣ (01) 887 2400 ⓦ www.morrisonhotel.ie ⓝ Bus: 16A to Dame St

Paramount Hotel ££ A busy hotel deep in the heart of Temple Bar but one which has rooms overlooking a central courtyard so the potential noise doesn't filter through. Breakfast, in the Turk's Head bar downstairs, can get busy too, so eat early. Plus, it's not far to wal or taxi home after a night out. ⓐ Parliament St & Essex Gate ⓣ (01) 417 9900 ⓦ www.paramounthotel.ie ⓝ Bus: 16A to Dame St

The Park Inn ££ Modern, breezy hotel with a good bar. Large, airy rooms with lots of facilities. ⓐ Smithfield ⓣ (01) 817 3838 ⓦ www.hoteldirect.co.uk/dublin ⓝ Luas: Smithfield

🔺 *Stay in celebratory style at The Clarence Hotel*

The Clarence Hotel £££ There just aren't enough pound signs to cover the rates at this stylish place, which is owned by Bono and The Edge of U2 fame. Leather lifts, over-the-top luxury in the rooms. Nice bar and restaurant and the occasional celebrity. ⓐ 6–8 Wellington Quay ⓣ (01) 407 0800 ⓦ www.theclarence.ie ⓝ Bus: 16A to Dame St

Clarion Hotel £££ Set in the IFSC area, this purpose-built, well-designed place is right on the riverfront, close to O'Connell Street and surrounded by the sandwich bars and cafés of the business district. Fitness centre, pool, nice bar food, good breakfast. ⓐ Excise Walk ⓣ (01) 433 8800 ⓦ www.clarionhotelifsc.com ⓝ Bus: 16A to O'Connell St

Dylan Hotel £££ The city's trendiest and most famous (boutique) hotel is located in a plush 19th-century town house. Services and facilities are what you'd expect – and then some – and judicious posing in the lounge offers great star-spotting opportunities. ⓐ Eastmoreland Place ⓣ (01) 660 3000 ⓦ www.dylan.ie ⓝ Aircoach

Stauntons on the Green £££ That would be the charming St Stephen's Green. This 3-star hotel has fantastically decorated rooms and fabulously attentive staff. ⓐ 83 St Stephen's Green ⓣ (01) 478 2300 ⓦ www.thecastlehotelgroup.com ⓝ Aircoach

HOSTELS

Avalon House Hostel £ If price is your main priority, this place is for you. Single and double rooms in a well-run hostel. Book early and be prepared for lots of noise. ⓐ 55 Aungier St ⓣ (01) 475 0001 ⓦ www.avalon-house.ie ⓝ Bus: 16A to Aungier St

The Brewery Hostel £ Out of the main tourist area, this is a quiet place with private rooms as well as dorm beds. ⓐ 22–23 Thomas St ⓣ (01) 453 8600 ⓦ www.irish-hostel.com ⓝ Bus: 123 to Thomas St

Kinlay House Christchurch £ Private rooms with shared or en suite bathrooms in this hostel. Laundry and kitchen make up for the lack of luxuries. ⓐ 2–12 Lord Edward St ⓣ (01) 679 6644 ⓦ www.kinlayhouse.ie ⓝ Bus: 16A to Dame St

Oliver St John Gogarty £ Smart hostel with private rooms, safe, kitchens, laundry, internet access. ⓐ 18–21 Anglesea St ⓣ (01) 671 1822 ⓦ www.gogartys.ie ⓝ Bus: 16A to Dame St

THE BEST OF DUBLIN

Whether you are on a flying visit to Dublin, or taking a more leisurely break, there are some sights that should not be missed.

TOP 10 ATTRACTIONS

- *The Book of Kells* Exquisite medieval illustrated manuscript housed in an excellent exhibition within Trinity College's Old Library (see page 60)

- **Christ Church Cathedral** Beautiful, medieval, mosaic floors, the tomb of Strongbow and a crypt full of treasures (see page 77)

- **St Patrick's Cathedral** The ancient rival to Christ Church where the Duke of Kildare chanced his arm (see page 108)

- **Guinness Storehouse** Panoramic views of the city and a pint of stout as well (see page 100)

- **A walk around Howth Head** Wheeling seabirds, rare plant life, old lighthouses and a bracing afternoon's walk ends up in the pretty seaside town of Howth (see page 116)

- **National Museum of Archaeology & History** Find out about Ireland's troubled past (see page 66)

- **A pub crawl down South Great George's Street to Camden Street** Start early, stop for dinner then head south, where the evenings get wilder (see page 70)

- **Francis Bacon's Studio at the Dublin City Gallery The Hugh Lane** This guy really had tidying-up issues. The studio, relocated from London, gives incredible and vivid insight into the artist's life, work and techniques (see page 90)

- **Malahide Castle** Find out how the wealthy landowners lived and maybe encounter the castle's ghost (see page 121)

- **The Viking Splash Tour** Throw self-respect and decorum to the wind, put on the Viking helmet and enjoy (see page 149)

🔽 *St Patrick's Cathedral*

Suggested itineraries

HALF-DAY: DUBLIN IN A HURRY

With a half-day in Dublin, the place to head for is the Guinness Storehouse (see page 100) where you can see the entire city in one go. From there head back to Temple Bar for an alfresco lunch while taking in the ambience.

1 DAY: TIME TO SEE A LITTLE MORE

With an entire day at your disposal, there is time to take in a couple more of the big sights, perhaps *The Book of Kells* (see page 60) or the National Museum of Archaeology & History (see page 66), with its displays of gold and the history of possibly Dublin's strangest and most unsettling time, the 1916 Uprising. Consider a picnic lunch in St Stephen's Green feeding the ducks and watching Dubliners taking a break. In the afternoon you could hit the Guinness Storehouse, and when you pour yourself out of there, quench the raging appetite that's

● *Watching over the River Liffey*

only too familiar to the connoisseur with a nosh-up at Monty's of Kathmandu (see page 81) in Temple Bar; or perhaps recuperate at Eliza Blue's (see page 81) with its views across the river and then just join in the fun of Temple Bar. Drifting as people do from one bar to the next and end the night by throwing a few shapes in one of the area's clubs.

2–3 DAYS: TIME TO SEE MUCH MORE

The two great ancient churches are worth visiting, and you will also have time to venture into north Dublin to visit Phoenix Park (see page 103), the Dublin Writer's Museum (see page 92) and the Dublin City Gallery The Hugh Lane (see page 90), and wander around the shopping streets of Henry Street, Moore Street and their tiny shopping centres and department stores. A day out on the DART is possible either to Howth in the north or Dun Laoghaire and points south, following the coastline on the now-ancient railway line. The nights can be filled with the glories of Temple Bar, a wander down the watering holes of South Great George's Street, or one of the many guided tours of ancient pubs. Venture out to Cobblestone (see page 113) for some authentic traditional music and try a meal at One Pico (see page 71) for a special night out.

LONGER: ENJOYING DUBLIN TO THE FULL

With more time to spend, you can enjoy a leisurely wander around the National Gallery (see page 66) or venture out to the Collins Barracks (see page 106), one of the biggest army barracks in Europe and now home to a branch of the National Museum. Your day trip could extend to Skerries (see page 124), a genuine seaside town with thatched roofs, a summer funfair and some elegant, great houses to explore. Best of all, consider taking one of the trips out to Newgrange Passage Tomb (see page 125), a Neolithic wonder of engineering.

Something for nothing

Ah, in what differing roles does capricious fate see fit to cast us! In these days of responsible spending, the once-reviled tightwad is king and what used to be termed psychopathic meanness has been re-themed as prudent husbandry of the domestic exchequer. Happily in these times of austerity, some of the best things to do in Dublin don't cost a penny.

The city itself is a sight to behold, with its intact Georgian squares such as Merrion Square or Mountjoy Square, where you can admire the elegant architectural details of the buildings. Lots of the squares have little parks which can afford you an hour or so of pleasant relaxation in the middle of your sightseeing day. Christ Church Cathedral (see page 77) has no admission charge, and if you enjoy churches you can visit the **Carmelite** (➋ 56 Aungier St), where St

IN FOR A PENNY? NO: IN FOR EVEN LESS

All of the following lure many a careful traveller with those honeyed words, 'free admission':

Chester Beatty Library (see page 77)
Dublin City Gallery The Hugh Lane (see page 90)
Irish Jewish Museum (see page 104)
Irish Museum of Modern Art (see page 104)
National Gallery (see page 66)
National Museum of Archaeology & History (see page 66)
National Museum of Decorative Arts & History at Collins Barracks (see page 106)
National Photographic Archive (see page 78)

○ *Visit the Georgian houses by the seaside in Bray*

Valentine's bones are kept, or **St Mary's Abbey** (ⓔ Meetinghouse Lane), a chapter house with an exhibition of medieval life.

If you discount the cost of the DART fare, a day trip out to the seaside at Bray (see page 131) will cost you nothing. The cliff walk at Howth (see page 116), too, costs nothing beyond structural damage to your coiffure, and doing a day or so of the Wicklow Way (see page 135) is a rewarding, if strenuous, way to not spend any money.

When it rains

The advent of rain in Dublin is barely noticed by its citizens, who just get out their umbrellas and carry on with what they were doing. For the visitor it might limit what you can do – Howth Head (see page 116) wouldn't be too much fun and neither would the Wicklow Way (see page 135). But the city has lots of indoor activities.

Shopping will keep you out of the rain for hours, especially if you keep to the shopping centres and big department stores. Another option is **The City Sightseeing Tour** (☎ (01) 605 7705), a hop-on, hop-off live commentary tour of the city which takes you to 20 different sights and will keep you dry (as long as you don't sit in the open-top upper deck). The buses are located outside the GPO in O'Connell Street (see page 48) and leave at 15-minute intervals.

The National Museum of Archaeology & History, with its hoards of gold (see page 66), and the National Gallery, with its Picasso and Caravaggio (see page 66), are but a quick dash away from each other and could easily fill a whole day.

Movie-watching always makes a good keeping-dry activity, and there are cinemas in Eustace Street, O'Connell Street, D'Olier Street and Parnell Street. Indoor sports also make a good activity for a rainy day. For controlled exposure to moisture, consider visiting a pool. You might consider taking the DART out to Malahide (see page 120); it's a pleasant journey and you can hop straight out of the train and into Malahide Castle (see page 121). The tour is excellent and afterwards there are other sights to visit inside the castle courtyard. Best of all on a rainy day perhaps is to find a warm café bar, say Bewley's Café Bar (see page 69), and linger over a coffee or something stronger while you smugly watch the people outside getting wet.

◆ Take a break at the Chester Beatty Library café

On arrival

TIME DIFFERENCE

Ireland is on GMT. During Daylight Saving Time (late Mar–late Oct), the clocks are put ahead one hour.

ARRIVING

By air

Dublin Airport (🕿 (01) 844 4900) is 12 km (7 ½ miles) north of the city. Its arrivals hall has a tourist office (see page 152) with money exchange facilities, left luggage, cash machines, car-hire booths, and a CIE counter which will provide information on bus services. (If you plan to hire a car you should do so before you leave your own country since there can be shortages in the summer.)

The journey from the airport into the city is by bus or taxi. **Dublin Bus** (🌐 www.dublinbus.ie) runs two bus services called the Airlink Express. The 747 travels directly to O'Connell Street, then to the **Busáras Central Bus Station** (🅰 Store St 🕿 (01) 836 6111 🌐 www.buseireann.ie) and Connolly Station (see opposite). The 748 takes in Tara St DART station, Aston Quay (for Temple Bar) and Heuston Station (for destinations in the south of the country, see opposite). **CIE** (🌐 www.cie.ie) sells prepaid tickets, single or return, or you can pay the bus driver.

The privately run **Aircoach** (🕿 (01) 844 7118 🌐 www.aircoach.ie) runs to Merrion Square and into Ballsbridge, stopping at designated points. It is useful for visitors staying south of the river. It picks up passengers in the access road in front of the arrivals hall. Another alternative is to use the regular public bus, numbers 41 and 41B to Eden Quay, or 16 and 16A to Aungier Street. They are less expensive but take much longer. They are useful for visitors staying in the north of the city.

By rail

Trains from Rosslare, Belfast and towns in Northern Ireland arrive at **Connolly Station** (ⓐ Amiens St ⓣ (01) 836 3333 ⓦ www.irishrail.ie). Connolly has left luggage facilities and connects with the DART and with Busáras via bus 90 from outside the station. There are also taxis available.

Trains from Cork, Galway, Westport, Tralee, Killarney, Limerick, Wexford and Waterford arrive at **Heuston Station** (ⓐ St John's Rd

⚫ *DART train in Tara Street Station*

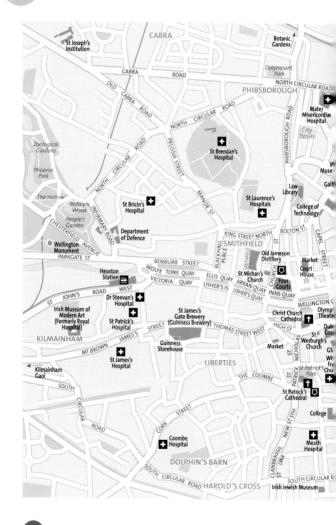

West ☎ (01) 677 1871 ⓦ www.irishrail.ie) in the west of the city. Heuston has left luggage facilities, ATM machines, shops and cafés and connects with the city centre via bus 90 and several local buses.

By road

Long-distance buses arrive at Busáras Central Bus Station (see page 48) from destinations around the country and from Northern Ireland. There are seven daily arrivals and departures from Belfast. Journey time is about three hours. Car drivers from Northern Ireland will arrive in the north of the city via the M1 motorway. Be aware that parking in the city is at a premium and most hotels do not have their own car parks.

By water

The **Stena ferry** (☎ (01) 204 7700) docks at Dun Laoghaire, from where foot passengers can take the DART or bus 7, 7A or 8 into the city. Drivers will find the route into the city signposted.

Dublin Port Bus 53 meets incoming ferries. Its destination is the central bus station. Taxis are also available.

FINDING YOUR FEET

Dublin is as safe a city as you can expect in Western Europe, perhaps a little safer than most. However, drug crime has increased and there is always the risk of mugging or bag snatching. ATM machines have entered the criminal repertoire with sophisticated gadgets reading PINs as they are keyed in, so choose an ATM in a public place and check that it doesn't look tampered with. Bear in mind, though, that while there are gun crimes reported on Irish radio on a weekly basis, this is because Ireland is a small country and there is little other news. It is common to hear on national radio news of a fight in Galway, for instance, where no one was seriously injured or arrested, or a car accident where someone was slightly injured.

For the newly arrived visitor to Ireland the chief problem with settling into the pace of life, even in Dublin, is learning to slow down. Hotels and B&Bs do breakfast often until 10.30; smaller shops and cafés open at 09.30 or later, and most of the museums get going at around 10.00. A major activity in the city is talking; complete strangers will gossip away at bus stops and your cab driver will

◔ A sightseeing tour is always a good way to see the city

lecture you on Dublin politics or winkle out of you all your family history, your Irish roots, where you've come from and where you're going. Where other cities offer great sights, art works or beautiful architecture as their main attractions, Dublin's greatest offer is its citizens, and to really enjoy life in Dublin you have to take the time to stop and chat wherever possible.

ORIENTATION

The city is divided rather neatly in two by the Liffey River, and to avoid confusion it is as well to bear in mind the compass points when travelling around. In the north of the city the central street is O'Connell Street. North of this is Parnell Square and to the west of it is Smithfield and Phoenix Park. To the east of O'Connell Street is the IFSC (International Financial Services Centre, see page 86), Custom House Visitor Centre (see page 86) and hotels along the river, and further east is the Point depot, then the river estuary.

The south of the river is dominated by Westmoreland Street and Grafton Street. To their west is the area known as the Liberties, where you can visit the Guinness Storehouse (see page 100) and Kilmainham Gaol (see page 105). East of the main thoroughfare are Temple Bar, Trinity College (see page 65) and Merrion Square. To the south of Grafton Street is the Grand Canal and beyond that Ballsbridge, where much of the accommodation can be found.

To the north of Dublin along the coastline of Dublin Bay is first Howth (see page 116), then Malahide (see page 120), then Skerries (see page 124), all accessible by DART or suburban rail. To the south is Dun Laoghaire (see page 128), Bray (see page 131) and then County Wicklow (see page 135).

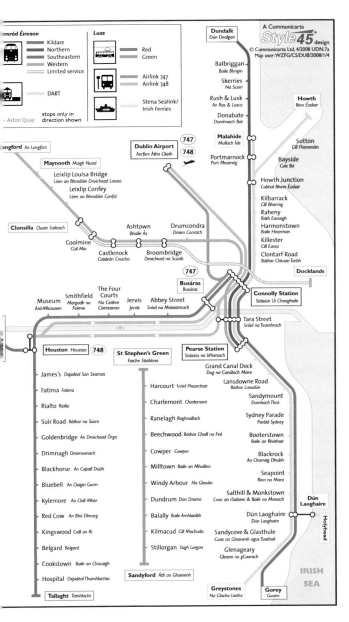

GETTING AROUND

Dublin is compact and the majority of sights and attractions as well as shopping areas can be reached on foot, which is by far the best way to experience the city. If your accommodation is outside the city centre or if you want to get to some of the outlying sights, you'll find the bus service is inexpensive and efficient.

Dublin Bus stops are painted yellow and usually have a timetable posted on them. The driver is paid on entry with the exact fare in coins. If you are uncertain as to the fare, the driver will tell you. If you don't have the exact change the driver will issue a receipt for the excess money and you can reclaim it at Dublin Bus in O'Connell Street. To find out the time of the next bus, just text 'bus' and the number of the bus required to ☏ 53503 and they will send you the next two or three buses in each direction.

There are several concessionary tickets which will make travelling around the city easier and slightly cheaper. The rambler ticket allows unlimited bus travel for 1, 3, 5 or 7 days. With a photo ID from Dublin Bus there are also concessionary tickets allowing a combination of bus and DART travel or bus and Luas, but unless you are staying for some time and intend to travel around the city a lot, they may not be worth the expense. There are also Family Bus Travel tickets allowing unlimited family travel on buses and DART. For details on all passes and other information, check ⓦ www.dublinbus.ie. Another option to consider is the Dublin Pass, offering free access to some tourist attractions, discounts in some cafés and shops and free transport on the Aircoach airport bus (see page 48). You'd have to work hard, though, to get your money's worth. The pass can be bought on-line at ⓦ www.dublinpass.ie

---

▶ *Statue of Molly Malone, the legendary fishmonger*

Luas trams (ⓦ www.luas.ie) are really for commuters but you could use it to get out to Collins Barracks (see page 106) and Smithfield and it's good fun. Tickets are bought at the stops from the machines. Singles are valid for an hour and return tickets last the day they are purchased.

The DART and suburban rail services travel along the coast to Skerries, Malahide, Howth, Dun Laoghaire and Bray, among other destinations. Tickets can be bought at the stations. DART stations in the city are Tara Street, Connolly Station and Pearse Street. The last DART trains out of Bray and Howth run at about midnight.

Taxi ranks are at St Stephen's Green, College Green and O'Connell Street.

Road driving or cycling around the city is not recommended. Few city hotels have car parks of their own so overnight parking can really put up your costs. There are no cycle lanes and few places where cycles can be left safely.

CAR HIRE

If you do choose to hire a set of wheels, the following are reliable firms:

easyCar Dublin ⓦ www.easycar.com/Dublin

Hertz ⓦ www.hertz.ie

Irish Car Rentals ⓦ www.irishcarrentals.com

▶ *The Famine Memorial on Custom House Quay*

Grafton Street & surrounding area

While the area north of the river spent the late 20th century sinking into decay and pound shops, the south side has always flourished. At its epicentre is Grafton Street, home to posh department stores and British chain stores. Settled all around is the seat of government, the big museums, some very exclusive hotels, St Stephen's Green and the fabulously expensive Georgian terraces of Merrion Square and its surrounds. Further south is the long road that starts off as South Great George's Street, turns into Aungier Street and becomes Wexford Street. This area has more pubs than you can shake a stick at. If you had only a couple of days in the city, there would be no need to venture across the river; most of what you want to see is tucked into this area and its tourist-dominated neighbour, Temple Bar.

SIGHTS & ATTRACTIONS

Bank of Ireland

Not normally on the must-see list for a visit to a city, this bank was once the old parliament building and still contains intact the Irish House of Lords, complete with tapestries, mace and all the other paraphernalia of Irish Protestant home rule. ⓐ College Green ⓘ (01) 677 6801 ⓛ Tours at 10.30, 11.30 & 13.45 Tues

The Book of Kells

Housed in the Old Library, a repository of three million or so books, *The Book of Kells* is a 9th-century illustrated manuscript of the four gospels. It had a turbulent life before it arrived in Trinity; stolen from the island of Iona by marauding Vikings, the book lost its probably gold- and precious-stone-clad bindings and several of the outer pages. You

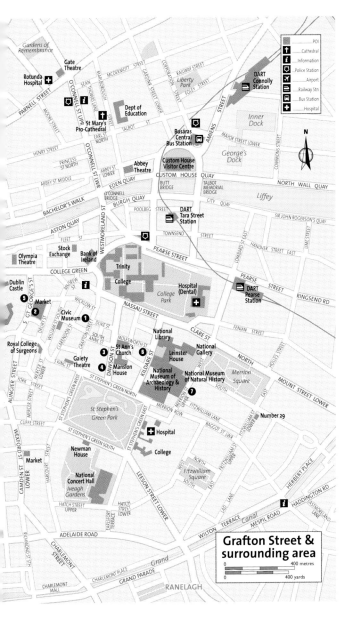

Grafton Street & surrounding area

view the manuscript itself inside a tiny glass case in a darkened room after wandering through an excellent exhibition on its manufacture and history. Afterwards you can wander through the rest of the library admiring the impressive collection housed here. ⓐ Old Library, Trinity College ⓘ (01) 896 2320 ⓦ www.tcd.ie ⓛ 09.30–17.00 Mon–Sat, 09.30–16.30 Sun, May–Sept; 09.30–17.00 Mon–Sat, 12.00–16.30 Sun, Oct–Apr, closed for ten days over Christmas. Admission charge

Merrion Square

Home to some of the most expensive real estate in the city, Merrion Square, built in 1762, was always where the really cool people lived, as you can see from the surfeit of blue plaques on the houses. Most famously, Oscar Wilde lived here with his parents and this is commemorated inside the little park with an ornate statue.

Newman House

These two Georgian buildings, home for a time to the Catholic University, are open to the public for guided tours only during the summer. The tour includes Gerard Manley Hopkins' rooms (he taught here in the final years of his life), the Apollo Room, where the glorious stucco plaster of the Lanfranchi brothers has been brought back to its original state, and a restored saloon where the Georgian gentry would once have played host to their friends. ⓐ 85–86 St Stephen's Green ⓘ (01) 716 7422 ⓛ Tours at 14.00, 15.00 & 16.00 Tues & Fri, June–Aug ⓝ Bus: 7, 10, 45; DART: Pearse St. Admission charge

Number 29

If you enjoy Georgiana then this more modest Georgian home is fun to visit. Research has turned up the original owners of the house and the tour includes details of their life, including the fascinating upstairs-

◯ *Statue of Oscar Wilde in Merrion Square*

SHEILA NA GIGS

In medieval times it was common for carved stone female figures to be inserted over the side doors of churches. These figures were seriously ugly, pulling wild faces and exposing their genitals to whomever looked up. One theory for this strange creature, the Sheila na gig, is that she was there to frighten off evil-doers from the church. Perhaps she stood as a warning to women to behave themselves. In more prudish times the Sheila na gigs were taken down from the church doorways and two of them have found their way into the room at the National Museum of Archaeology & History (see page 66) which holds the famous gold Ardagh Chalice.

downstairs relationship. The whole house is furnished with items from the archives of the National Museum, so it looks just as the original family would have had it. ❸ 29 Fitzwilliam St Lower ❶ (01) 702 6165 ❸ 10.00–17.00 Tues–Sat, 12.00–17.00 Sun, closed for two weeks before Christmas ❹ Bus: 7, 10, 45; DART: Pearse St. Admission charge

St Stephen's Green

If one part of the city can be said to summarise Dublin's existence, it is St Stephen's Green. Public grazing area, public hanging site, home to the strolling middle classes, site of one of the fiercest battles of the 1916 Uprising and now repository of all the commemorative detritus of several hundred years of fighting. There is also a nice park with a duck pond and benches where you can enjoy a picnic. Seek out the bust of Countess Markeivicz, one of the few unsung women heroes of the Uprising.

Trinity College

Established by Queen Elizabeth I in an effort to keep the young and impressionable sons of the Protestant ascendancy away from the vices of Europe, Trinity was for centuries a little bastion of Protestant education. Until 1970 the Catholic Church actually forbade Catholic students from attending the place. Inside the gates is a little haven of quiet learning (or it would be, except for the students and the hordes of tourists visiting *The Book of Kells*). Admire the architecture (most of which is Georgian rather than Elizabethan) and lovely squares, but follow the crowds to the real draw, *The Book of Kells*. The Dublin Experience, a multimedia presentation on the history of the city, is in the Arts Building here. ⊜ College Green ⊕ (01) 896 2320 ⓦ www.tcd.ie

The Dublin Experience ⊜ Arts Building, Trinity College ⊕ 10.00–19.00 May–Oct. Admission charge

⬣ *Trinity College*

CULTURE

National Gallery

Considering how small and poor Ireland was until the 1990s, this collection is quite impressive. Its contents are strong on Italian art, with Mantegna, Titian, Tintoretto, Fra Angelico and Caravaggio (the *Taking of Christ* was discovered in the 1990s hanging on a wall in Leeson Street) all making an appearance. There are also works by Rembrandt and Vermeer from the Dutch school and a Spanish collection that includes Velázquez, El Greco and Picasso. The Irish collection is well worth checking out, with a wing dedicated to Jack Yeats. ⊖ Merrion Square West & Clare St ⊕ (01) 661 5133 Ⓦ www.nationalgallery.ie ⊕ 09.30–17.30 Mon–Sat (till 20.30 Thurs), 12.00–17.30 Sun, closed bank holidays. Admission charge for special exhibitions

National Museum of Archaeology & History

The building itself is worth the visit but once inside past the beautiful entrance hall, check out the hoards of gold unearthed from Irish bogs over the years, the exhibition on the 1916 Uprising, and the upper floors with Viking and medieval exhibits. ⊖ Kildare St ⊕ (01) 677 7444 Ⓦ www.museum.ie ⊕ 10.00–17.00 Tues–Sat, 14.00–17.00 Sun ⊗ Bus: 7, 7A, 8 (from Burgh Quay), 10, 11, 13 (from O'Connell St); DART: Pearse St

RETAIL THERAPY

Grafton Street is a little enclave of British chain stores, but in between those are some home-grown department stores, and the St Stephen's Green Shopping Centre (see page 22) has some interesting shops in its upper floors. Around Kildare Street are the real treasures of Irish shopping; just about every small art and crafts centre in Ireland is represented around here. Between Grafton Street and South Great George's Street are lots of little classy clothes shops, antiques shops and more. Vintage clothes fans will enjoy a trek along South Great George's Street, Aungier Street and Camden Street for the multitude of charity shops (and a few places which actually call themselves vintage clothes shops and charge more for the service).

⬥ *Have a rummage through a bookshop*

A Wear Lots of Irish designers at affordable prices. 🅰 26 Grafton St
ℹ️ (01) 671 7200 🕐 09.00–18.00 Mon–Wed, Fri & Sat, 09.00–20.00
Thur, 13.00–18.00 Sun

Brown Thomas Old-school, posh department store. Go to look
and admire. Lots of designer threads. 🅰 88–92 Grafton St
ℹ️ (01) 605 6666 🕐 09.00–18.00 Mon–Wed, Fri & Sat,
09.00–20.00 Thur, 12.00–18.00 Sun

Camden Street Market Fruit, veg, flowers and cheap clothes.
🕐 09.00–17.00 Mon–Sat

George's Street Arcade Covered market full of vintage clothes,
books, CDs and inexpensive jewellery. Good café. 🕐 09.00–19.00

The Kilkenny Store Lovely, lovely things on two floors from little
craft shops all over the country, plus a great café. 🅰 6 Nassau St
ℹ️ (01) 677 7066 🌐 www.kilkennygroup.com 🕐 09.00–19.00
Mon–Sat

Magill's Delicatessen All you need for a picnic lunch. 🅰 14 Clarendon St
ℹ️ (01) 671 3830 🕐 09.00–17.00 Mon–Sat

Powerscourt Centre Classy shopping centre with not a chain store
in sight. Lots of antiques, designer clothes, jewellery, kooky t-shirts
and more. 🅰 59 South William St ℹ️ (01) 679 4144 🕐 09.00–18.00
Mon–Wed, Fri & Sat, 09.00–20.00 Thur, 12.00–18.00 Sun

Rhinestones Possibly the nicest shop in Dublin. Antique jewellery
of all kinds from the real thing to 1940s funky junk. 🅰 18 Andrew St

ⓘ (01) 679 0759 🕒 09.30–18.00 Mon–Wed, Fri & Sat,
09.30–20.00 Thur

Sheridan's Cheesemonger Lots of interesting cheeses
from Ireland and abroad. 🅰 11 South Anne St ⓘ (01) 679 3143
Ⓦ www.sheridanscheesemongers.com 🕒 09.00–17.00 Mon–Sat

TAKING A BREAK

Bewley's Café Bar £ ❶ For 160 years this place served tea and
crumpets and fry-ups to the populace of Dublin, but in 2005 amidst
great sighs and wailings it closed its doors... only to reopen in the

⬥ Bewley's, a great little day or night-spot

guise of a café bar. It's seriously affordable, family-orientated and offers modern cuisine with pizzas and pastas and innovative salad. There is occasionally lunchtime theatre, but don't let that put you off. While you're there check out the stained-glass windows by Harry Clark. ⓐ Bewley's Building, Grafton St ⓣ (01) 672 7720 ⓦ www.bewleys.ie ⓛ 12.00–22.00 Sun–Wed, 12.00–23.00 Thur–Sat

Café Bar Deli £ ❷ Nice Mediterranean food, pleasant surroundings; come back at night for the music. ⓐ 12–13 South Great George's St ⓣ (01) 677 1646 ⓛ 12.30–23.00 Mon–Sat, 14.00–22.00 Sun

Café en Seine £ ❸ Seriously over-the-top designer bar. Very affordable modern food. Jazz on Sunday afternoons and jazz band on Monday nights. ⓐ 39–40 Dawson St ⓣ (01) 677 4567 ⓦ www.capitalbars.com ⓛ 11.00–03.00

Fitzers £ ❹ One of the most welcoming places in the city to drop in for a daytime dip into a menu that's absolutely full of Italian goodies. ⓐ 51 Dawson St ⓣ (01) 671 1559 ⓦ www.fitzers.ie ⓛ 09.00–23.00

Juice £ ❺ This is as good as it gets for vegetarians in this city: macrobiotic restaurant, inexpensive lunches and funny-sounding drinks. ⓐ 73 South Great George's St ⓣ (01) 475 7856 ⓦ www.juicerestaurant.ie ⓛ 12.00–22.00 Mon–Wed, 12.00–23.00 Thur & Fri, 10.00–23.00 Sat, 10.00–22.00 Sun

AFTER DARK

If you enjoy pub crawls you might like to check out the Dublin Literary Pub Crawl, which starts out in The Duke (Duke Street) and, along with some actors and storytellers, wanders the more literary pubs of the city. This happens nightly at 19.30 (book in advance on ☏ (01) 670 5602 ⓦ www.dublinpubcrawl.com). Alternatively you can manufacture your own, possibly less literary one, by starting at the top of South Great George's Street and working your way down.

RESTAURANTS

One Pico £££ ❻ Service is excellent but then you are paying for it in this well-run, spacious, modern dining room. If you enjoy modern cooking at its best, make this the place you splash out on during your visit. ⓐ Molesworth Place ☏ (01) 676 0300 ⓦ www.onepico.com ⏱ 12.30–14.30, 19.30–22.30 Mon–Sat, 19.30–22.00 Sun

Pearl Brasserie £££ ❼ Upmarket basement restaurant serving original, thoughtful French/Irish cuisine; foie gras and shellfish feature strongly. Lots of pillars give a sense of privacy. There's a nice bar area to settle in before eating, and good service. ⓐ 20 Merrion St Upper ☏ (01) 661 3572 ⓦ www.pearl-brasserie.com ⏱ 12.30–14.30, 17.30–22.30 Mon–Sat

PUBS & CLUBS

The Bailey Famous pub where Brendan Behan used to drink. By day it fills with shoppers and workers and has a huge lunch menu; by night it chills out a little and intellectuals with coughs get their nicotine fixes at the pavement tables. ⓐ 2 Duke St ☏ (01) 670 4939 ⓦ www.baileybar.ie ⏱ 11.30–23.30 (till 00.30 Sat)

Carnival Cool dark interior on two levels. Very popular bar with a party atmosphere and no cover charge. ⓐ 11 Wexford St ☏ (01) 405 3604

Davy Byrne's The famous pub that Leopold Bloom calls into in *Ulysses*. Always crowded with tourists and city folk. ⓐ 21 Duke St ⓣ (01) 677 5217 ⓦ www.davybyrnes.com ⓛ 11.30–23.30 (till 00.30 Sat)

Gaiety Theatre This is actually a theatre, but on Friday and Saturday nights (if there is no opera or ballet on), the place turns into a live music venue with salsa, jazz or soul. Attracts an older crowd. ⓐ South King St ⓣ (01) 677 1717 ⓛ Variable, so phone to check

The Globe A relatively tranquil place in the boozing maelstrom, and thus a fine venue for thinking through your priorities before heading out to get slaughtered. ⓐ 11 South Great George's St ⓣ (01) 671 1220 ⓦ www.globe.ie ⓛ 12.00–03.00 Mon–Sat, 12.00–23.00 Sun

Hogan's Two levels; the ground floor is, during the day, a pleasant café bar with huge windows open to the street where you can watch the world going by; the basement opens late and rocks. ⓐ 35 South Great George's St ⓣ (01) 677 5904 ⓛ 12.30–23.30 Mon–Wed, 12.30–00.30 Thur, 10.30–02.30 Fri & Sat, 15.00–23.00 Sun

The International Nice old pub full of character, with a club upstairs. Live jazz, blues or folk most nights. ⓐ 23 Wicklow St ⓣ (01) 677 9250 ⓛ 11.30–23.30 (till 00.30 Sat)

J J Smyth's A once-basic pub that's flowered into a jazz and blues club, too. ⓐ 12 Aungier St ⓣ (01) 475 2565 ⓦ www.jjsmyths.com ⓛ 12.00 until gigs finish

Lillie's Bordello Still going strong after all these years. Fussy doormen, though. Dress up for this place; A-listers will be here. ⓐ Grafton St

🕿 (01) 679 9204 🌐 www.lilliesbordello.ie 🕒 23.00–02.30 Mon–Sat, 22.00–01.00 Sun

Lobby Bar/POD/Red Box/Craw Daddy The coolest places to be in Dublin after midnight. Who cares about celebrities when everyone looks so good? Four clubs all in one building. The Redbox is for throwing yourself around, POD for live acts, Craw Daddy and the Lobby Bar for looking serene. 🚇 Old Harcourt St Station, Harcourt St 🕿 (01) 661 0700 🕒 Variable for all four venues, so phone the main number to check

Long Hall Long, beautiful, old Victorian pub, no gimmicks or modish design features; just as it was a hundred years ago. 🚇 51 South Great George's St 🕿 (01) 475 1590 🕒 16.00–23.30 Mon–Wed, 13.00–23.00 Thur, 13.00–00.30 Fri & Sat, 16.00–23.00 Sun

O'Donoghues One of the best places to go for impromptu traditional Irish sessions, but it can get very crowded with locals and tourists. 🚇 15 Merrion Row 🕿 (01) 660 7194 🌐 www.odonoghues.ie 🕒 10.30–23.30 Mon–Wed, 10.30–00.30 Thur–Sat, 12.30–23.00 Sun

The Sugar Club Very sophisticated place built in an old sugar factory. Live music most nights and occasional comedy nights. Lots of different bars to enjoy in one place. 🚇 Leeson St Lower 🕿 (01) 678 7188 🌐 www.thesugarclub.com 🕒 Variable depending on event, so phone the main number to check

Whelan's Live music every night in this long-established bar. 🚇 25 Wexford St 🕿 (01) 478 0766 🕒 10.30–00.00

Temple Bar & surrounding area

Twenty years ago this area, between the river and Dame Street and from Fishamble Street to Fleet Street, was derelict, full of crazy little shops selling second-hand clothes, alternative music and the like, but as the Celtic Tiger cub grew to maturity, this place metamorphosed into the tourist-dedicated hotspot it is today. For all the blarney handed out, there is some genuine non-manufactured nightlife here (possibly a little too much on a Friday night when the hen parties are roaming) and good shops and places to visit. Around the perimeter of Temple Bar are some of the really big sights. After dark Temple Bar gives itself over entirely to fun. The pubs spill out onto the streets, the tourist shops open late, restaurants fill up and as the night wears on the clubs upstairs in the bars get going. At lunchtime every pub in the place has pub food, many have live music of some sort, and a considerable number have huge TV screens with some testosterone-driven activity showing. Check out ⓦ www.templebar.ie for details of free concerts and performances in Temple Bar.

SIGHTS & ATTRACTIONS

City Hall

This handsome, 18th-century building was once the Royal Exchange. After 1801, when Dublin began its big decline, the building was no longer needed and it became an administrative centre. In the basement is an exhibition on the history of the city but it's worth popping in just for the stunning rotunda with its 5.5-m (18-ft) statue of Daniel O'Connell (no, not Daniel O'Donnell). ⓐ Dame St ⓣ (01) 222 2204 ⓦ www.dublincity.ie ⓛ 10.00–17.15 Mon–Sat, 14.00–17.00 Sun & bank holidays ⓝ Bus: 77, 77A, 56A, 49 (from Eden Quay), 123 (from O'Connell St). Admission charge

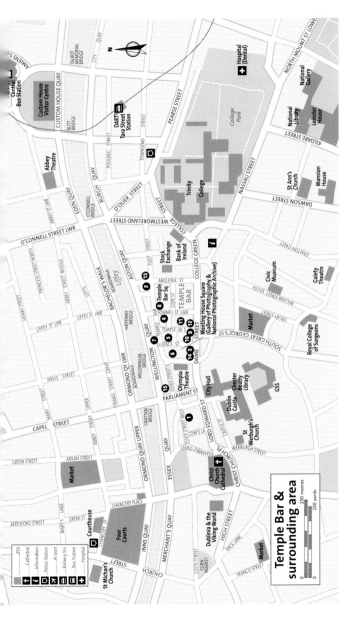

Meeting House Square

Not quite a Mediterranean piazza, but it's getting there. The square
is home to a Sunday morning farmers' market where you can buy
lumpy carrots and organic honey as well as some more esoteric stuff.
In summer the square doubles as an open-air cinema and when it's
warm enough the cafés that surround the square put out tables.

◯ The Statue of Justice keeps watch over the city

CULTURE

Chester Beatty Library

Chester Beatty was a seriously rich American with a tenuous link to Ireland who left his enormous collection of ancient manuscripts to the Irish state. For years it festered out in the sticks, but in 2000 it was brought into the city in all its glory. Well worth a visit. ❸ Dublin Castle, Dame St ❶ (01) 407 0750 ❷ 10.00–17.00 Mon–Fri, 11.00–17.00 Sat, 13.00–17.00 Sun, closed Mon in winter

Christ Church Cathedral

Bits of this ancient building were erected in the 11th century when Dublin was a Viking city. Most of what you see is a Victorian make-over, including the tomb of Strongbow (the Norman conqueror of Ireland), but the place has a quality of its own. There is a museum of gold and silver bits and pieces in the crypt, and the floor tiles, replicas of the damaged medieval originals, are beautiful. ❸ Christ Church Place ❶ (01) 677 8099 ❿ www.cccdub.ie ❷ 09.00–18.00 June–Aug; 09.45–17.00 Sept–May ❺ Bus: 49, 50, 51B, 54A, 56A, 65, 77, 77A, 78A, 123; DART: Tara St, then Bus: 90. Admission charge for crypt

Dublin Castle

The place where Dublin castle now stands was once a strategic location where the River Poddle (now underground) met the Liffey and a fort has stood here since early Christian times. The building you see before you is a more modern construct, now used when Ireland chairs the EU for official meetings. A visit here involves a very entertaining tour; the guides take you around the various sumptuous rooms and corridors, with graphic stories of the history of each room, and end up in the undercroft where you can make out the remains of the original

fortifications. ⓐ Dame St ❶ (01) 645 8813 Ⓦ www.dublincastle.ie
🕐 10.00–16.45 Mon–Fri, 14.00–16.45 Sat, Sun & public holidays ⓝ Bus: 77,
77A, 56A, 49 (from Eden Quay), 123 (from O'Connell St). Admission charge

Gallery of Photography

The gallery has a permanent collection of 20th-century Irish
photographs plus some excellent changing exhibitions. ⓐ Meeting
House Square ❶ (01) 671 4654 Ⓦ http://galleryofphotography.ie
🕐 11.00–18.00 Tues–Sat, 13.00–18.00 Sun

National Photographic Archive

The National Library's collection of 600,000 photographs contains
both historical and contemporary photographs, with subjects ranging
from the political to the topographic. ⓐ Meeting House Square
❶ (01) 603 0371 Ⓦ www.nli.ie 🕐 10.00–17.00 Mon–Fri

DUBLINIA & THE VIKING WORLD

For a completely manufactured tourist destination, this is
definitely one of the best. Set inside the old Synod Hall and
linked to Christ Church Cathedral via an overhead bridge, the
exhibition re-creates the sights, sound and smells of medieval
and Viking Dublin. At the end of the exhibition you can climb
to the top of St Michael's tower for stunning views over the
city. ⓐ St Michael's Hill ❶ (01) 679 4611 Ⓦ www.dublinia.ie
🕐 10.00–17.00 Apr–Sept; 11.00–16.00 Mon–Sat, 10.00–16.00
Sun & bank holidays, Oct–Mar ⓝ Bus: 50 (from Eden Quay),
78A (from Aston Quay); Luas: Red Line (from Four Courts).
Admission charge

RETAIL THERAPY

Once a bohemian, counter-culture ghetto, Temple Bar is now the place to go for a variety of gorgeous, if expensive, items, as well as some trashy get-it-for-the-in-laws stuff.

Amnesty International Shop Books, Fair-Trade products, nice coffee bar and internet connection. The big plus? That inner glow of smugness. ⓐ 48 Fleet St ⓣ (01) 677 6361 ⓛ 09.00–17.30 Mon–Sat

The House of Astrology Tarot cards, aromatherapy oils, tumblestones, relaxation CDs, hypnosis tapes, books on astrology, tarot, alternative healing and more. ⓐ 9 Parliament St ⓣ (01) 679 3404 ⓦ www.houseofastrology.com ⓛ 10.00–18.00 Mon–Sat

Irish Celtic Craftshop Some good Irish designs in jewellery. ⓐ 10–12 Lord Edward St ⓣ (01) 679 9912 ⓛ 10.00–18.00 Mon–Sat

Meeting House Square Organic farmers' market. Everything's pesticide free, and the chickens who laid the eggs at least had a chance to stretch their legs a bit. ⓐ Meeting House Square ⓛ 08.00–14.00 Sat

Temple Bar Fashion Market Unique, one-off garments from some prestigious up-and-coming young Dubliners, children's wear, avant-garde and interesting objects, elegant handbags, purses and original accessories, hand-made and Italian resin jewellery and hand-blocked t-shirts. ⓐ Cow's Lane ⓛ 10.00–17.30 Sat

Temple Bar Jewellers Some pretty pieces of jewellery in traditional and modern designs. ❸ 27 Eustace St ❶ (01) 677 3647 Ⓦ www.glycine.ie ◷ 09.00–17.30 Mon–Sat

Temple Wear Small, trendy clothes shop. ⓐ 3 Fownes St Upper ❶ (01) 671 5253 ◷ 09.30–17.30 Mon–Sat

TAKING A BREAK

The Bakery £ ❶ Lovely cakes, filled rolls and pastries to take out for a picnic or eat in with a coffee. ❸ Unit 3 Pudding Row, Essex St West ❶ (01) 672 9882 ◷ 07.00–18.00 Mon–Fri, 07.00–17.00 Sat

Gallagher's Boxty House £ ❷ The place to try out this traditional Irish dish – potato pancakes filled with all manner of good things. ⓐ 20–21 Temple Bar ❶ (01) 677 2762 Ⓦ www.boxtyhouse.ie ◷ 08.30–23.30 Mon–Fri, 09.00–23.30 Sat, 10.00–23.30 Sun

Gruel £ ❸ Very popular, inexpensive, bare place serving soup and rolls as well as more substantial dishes. Good for lunch or an early evening eat-and-go kind of meal. ❸ 68a Dame St ❶ (01) 670 7119 ◷ 11.30–22.00 Mon–Sat, 11.30–21.00 Sun

Luigi Malone's £ ❹ Vast menu in a huge dining room with everything from pizzas to fajitas, ribs, burgers, fish and chips. Very popular at lunchtime. ❸ 5-6 Cecilia St, off Fownes St Lower ❶ (01) 679 2723 Ⓦ www.luigimalones.com ◷ 12.00–23.00

Bruno's £–££ ❺ French restaurant with a great buzz and great service. The food's absolutely top notch, too. ❸ Eustace St ❶ (01) 670 6767 Ⓦ www.brunosdublin.com ◷ 12.00–23.00

Eden ££ ❻ A great place for an evening meal but just as good for an afternoon coffee or lunch. Modern Irish cuisine. ⓐ Meeting House Square ❶ (01) 670 5372 ❺ 12.30–15.00, 18.00–22.30 Mon–Fri, 19.00–23.00 Sat

Eliza Blue's ££ ❼ Some good lunch specials in this modern place with floor-to-ceiling windows overlooking the river. Good seafood options. ⓐ 23 Wellington Quay ❶ (01) 671 9114 ❺ 07.30–15.00, 17.00–23.00 Mon–Fri, 08.00–16.00, 17.00–23.00 Sat & Sun

Fitzer's ££ ❽ Hot, filled rolls and burgers. No relation to the one on Dawson Street. ⓐ Temple Bar Square ❶ (01) 679 0440 ❺ 12.00–23.30

Tante Zoe's ££ ❾ Cajun and Creole delights such as jambalaya and blackened chicken are served up with aplomb in this busy – yet relaxed – joint. ⓐ 1 Crow St, off Dame St ❶ (01) 679 4407 ⓦ www.tantezoes.com ❺ 12.00–24.00 Mon–Sat, 16.00–22.00 Sun

AFTER DARK

RESTAURANTS
Monty's of Kathmandu £ ❿ One menu all day long so dinner doesn't suddenly become pricier than lunch. Lovely authentic Nepalese food, cooked in one of the most long-standing and well-established restaurants. Monty's was here before Temple Bar became cool. Try their own-label beer. ⓐ 28 Eustace St ❶ (01) 670 4911 ❺ 12.00–14.30, 18.00–23.30 Mon–Sat, 11.00–23.30 Sun

FXB Temple Bar ££ ⓫ Seriously meat-centred menu with free-range animals dished up by weight. Fish and vegetarian options, too. Good early-bird menu. ⓐ 2 Crow St, off Dame St ⓣ (01) 671 1248 ⓦ www.fxbrestaurants.com ⓛ 17.30–23.00 Mon–Sat, 17.30–22.00 Sun

Nico's ££ ⓬ Long-established Italian restaurant. White tablecloths, busy waiters but – sadly – no Chianti bottles. ⓐ 53 Dame St

Enjoy a good meal at the Mermaid Café

ⓣ (01) 677 3062 ⓛ 12.30–15.00, 18.30–23.00 Mon–Sat, 12.00–15.30, 18.00–21.00 Sun

Oliver St John Gogarty's ££ ⓭ Irish stew, huge bowls of mussels, copper things hanging on the walls and fiddly-diddly music piped up from the bar downstairs. A bit cramped but bursting to the seams with satisfied customers. Reservations recommended, particularly at weekends. ⓐ 58–59 Fleet St ⓣ (01) 671 1822 ⓛ 12.00–23.00 Mon–Sat, 16.00–23.00 Sun

Mermaid Café £££ ⓮ Nouvelle American cuisine in this popular place with very reasonable prices given the quality of the food. ⓐ 69–70 Dame St ⓣ (01) 670 8236 ⓦ www.mermaid.ie ⓛ 12.30–15.00, 18.30–23.00 Mon–Sat, 12.00–15.30, 18.00–21.00 Sun

The Tea Room £££ ⓯ If you can't afford to stay at the Clarence you should eat here. The Tea Room offers excellent modern Irish cooking in an almost austere but elegant, refectory-style dining room. Very popular Sunday brunch. ⓐ Clarence Hotel, 6–8 Wellington Quay ⓣ (01) 670 7766 ⓦ www.theclarence.ie ⓛ 12.30–15.00, 18.30–23.00

PUBS & CLUBS
Club M Seriously dedicated nightclub with mirror balls and everything. DJs six nights a week. ⓐ Cope St ⓣ (01) 671 5622 ⓦ www.clubm.ie ⓛ 20.00–02.00 Mon–Sat

Fitzsimons Everything you ever dreamed would be in a pub – DJs, food, upstairs club, big-screen telly. Oh, and booze. ⓐ Temple Bar ⓦ www.fitzsimonshotel.com ⓛ 11.00–23.00

Front Lounge Wine bar where all the really cool people hang out. Occasional live music and comedy nights. 🅰 33–34 Parliament St 🄣 (01) 670 4112 🄛 12.00–23.00 Mon–Wed & Sun, 12.00–01.30 Thur–Sat

Ha'penny Bridge Named after the bridge that it looks out on, this pub is best known for its open mic comedy night. 🅰 42 Wellington Quay 🄛 11.30–23.00

Octagon The bar where Bono sat and dreamed his dreams over a Guinness or two is now ultra sleek and a good place for cocktails. 🅰 6–8 Wellington Quay 🄣 (01) 407 0800 🅦 www.theclarence.ie 🄛 10.00–23.00 Mon–Sat, 12.30–22.30 Sun

Turk's Head Good place for a knees-up. Very tourist-oriented, garish bar, occasional live music – all in all, sublime. 🅰 27–30 Parliament St 🄣 (01) 679 9701 🄛 16.30–02.00

Viperoom Live lounge music seven nights in the bar and DJs doing their thing in the club upstairs. 🅰 5 Aston Quay 🄣 (01) 672 5566 🄛 12.30–01.30

THEATRES & CINEMAS

The Ark Children's theatre workshop that has regular programmes of highly entertaining shows. 🅰 11a Eustace St 🄣 (01) 670 7788 🅦 www.ark.ie

Irish Film Institute Independent foreign and low-budget Irish movies. 🅰 6 Eustace St 🄣 (01) 679 5744 🅦 www.irishfilm.ie 🄛 Booking from 13.30 daily

Olympia Theatre Dublin's surviving music hall where an enormous variety of productions take place. Worth checking out for the atmosphere. 🄰 72 Dame St 🄣 (01) 679 3323 🄦 www.olympia.ie

Project Arts Centre Two theatre spaces and a studio offer the city's most experimental theatre, art exhibitions, dance, regular live music, video and film. Also a nice bar. 🄰 39 Essex St East 🄣 (01) 679 6622 🄦 www.project.ie

🔺 *The unusual mosaic entrance to the Turk's Head*

O'Connell Street & surrounding area

For many years, this was the downmarket part of the city where, even while the Celtic Tiger roared, buildings stood derelict and pound shops ruled. The area has seen great transformations in the last few years, with the Monument of Light replacing some pretty rubbishy statuary and the derelict quays turning into bijou housing for the upwardly mobile. The now well-established IFSC (International Financial Services Centre) is here with a few good places to eat, some shops, but a chiefly residential and business tone. North of O'Connell Street is some good, inexpensive accommodation and O'Connell Street itself is a historic part of the city where the major battle of the 1916 Uprising was waged; the bullet scars are still evident.

SIGHTS & ATTRACTIONS

Boardwalk

Part of the effort to bring the north area of Dublin into the economic boom enjoyed by the rest of the city is the Boardwalk, which provides a pedestrian walkway along the north shore of the river where once only traffic heaved and blared. It is quite a pleasant walk, with benches for contemplating the nature of life in the city, and creates a link with Temple Bar across the road. It's a good place for a picnic lunch.

Custom House Visitor Centre

This is the place where in the old days ships had to park and declare what they were carrying and pay customs duties. When it was built in the 18th century, the merchants around Temple Bar tried to blow it up since its construction meant that their business, further up the

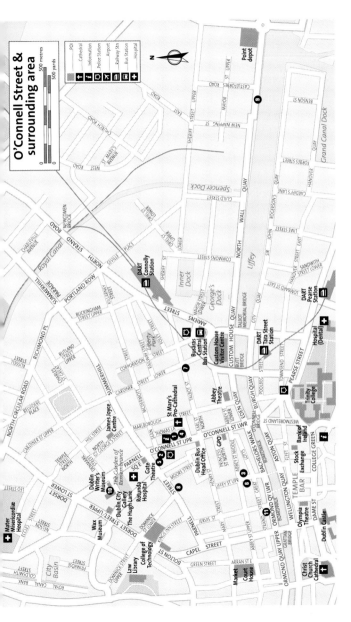

> **HUGH WHO?**
> When the *Lusitania* was torpedoed off the coast of
> County Cork in 1915, it left a pretty puzzle behind for the two
> governments of Britain and Ireland. Hugh Lane, the nephew
> of the Irish nationalist Lady Gregory, was on board and his will
> left his art collection to the state, which technically in 1915 was
> Britain. When Irish independence came in 1921, a quarrel arose
> over which state exactly he had meant. A partial resolution
> came in 1960 when the two governments agreed to share the
> collection, swapping stuff occasionally, but in 1968 Britain
> claimed the lot. The dispute was settled, again, by breaking up
> the collection, with half remaining permanently the property
> of the Irish state.

river, would disappear. In 1921 the building was caught up in the civil
war and was badly damaged. For many years an administrative centre,
the place has recently had a facelift and contains an exhibition of
the colourful history of the building and the city it serves. ❸ Custom
House Quay ❶ (01) 888 2538 ❸ 10.00–12.30 Mon–Fri, 14.00–17.00 Sat
& Sun ⓝ DART: Tara St. Admission charge

O'Connell Street

No mere A-to-B thoroughfare, no anonymous urban walkway, this
venerable street is a historical sight in itself. Until 1966, when the IRA
blew it up, a giant statue of Lord Nelson stood here. It was followed
by an ugly water feature called Anna Livia ('the spirit of the Liffey'),
which has been retired to a warehouse and replaced by the *Monument
of Light*, or whatever they're calling it this year (locals call it the 'stiletto

in the ghetto'), a 120-m (393-ft) illuminated pole that was supposed to be completed for the millennium but didn't make it in time. At the heart of the street is the GPO, which became the headquarters of the Easter Rising and which was gutted, as were most of the other buildings around it, by shells from a British gunboat moored in the Liffey. If you stand under the portico of the building and peer upwards, some of the bullet holes are still preserved there (you can also see bullet holes in the statue of Daniel O'Connell, after whom the street was named, at the head of the street). Nearby are the city's indigenous

🔼 *Rest those legs by the River Liffey*

department stores, while along Moore Street is an open-air market. In Cathedral Street is St Mary's Pro-Cathedral, built in 1825, well out of sight of the British rulers of the time.

Parnell Square & The Garden of Remembrance

As Dublin decayed during the first 80 years of the 20th century, many of its beautiful Georgian buildings became derelict, but this square, one of the first of a big building spree in the 18th century, remains intact. Central is the Garden of Remembrance (1966) where the statue *Children of Lir* commemorates those who died in the struggle for independence. Originally a pleasure garden where the gentry paid to stroll about, the income from it went into building the Rotunda Maternity Hospital, the first maternity hospital in Europe, which still functions today.

CULTURE

Dublin City Gallery The Hugh Lane

Once upon a time this grand building in the centre of the north side of Parnell Square was the most des res in Dublin, built for the Earl of Charlemont in 1762. It currently houses the city's collection of modern Irish and European art. Entrance is free and for that you get works by Corot, Monet, Degas, Manet and Burne Jones, as well as a sound collection of works by Irish painters such as Sarah Purser, Jack Yeats and the artist who worked in stained glass, Harry Clarke. The highlight of a visit to the gallery, though, is the (not so free) workshop of Francis Bacon which was relocated here from London, every last paintbrush and beer bottle faithfully replaced. ⓐ Charlemont House, Parnell Square

---

◗ Children of Lir: *another symbol of Ireland's historical struggles*

🕿 (01) 874 1903 Ⓦ www.hughlane.ie 🕓 09.30–18.00 Tues–Thur,
09.30–17.00 Fri & Sat, 11.00–17.00 Sun Ⓝ Bus: 3, 10, 11, 13, 16, 19.
Admission charge for the Francis Bacon workshop

Dublin Writer's Museum

Anyone who has studied English Literature in any depth will be
all too aware that a sizeable number of the really big names in
Eng Lit are actually Irish – Joyce, Beckett, Yeats, Shaw, Swift, Heaney,
Sheridan, Wilde and Behan, to name some of the heavyweights.
This museum pays homage to many of these great white males
with rare first editions, bits of their stuff, photographs and more,
all set in another of the beautiful Georgian town houses in Parnell
Square, a sight in itself. 🖈 18 Parnell Square 🕿 (01) 872 2077
Ⓦ www.visitdublin.com 🕓 10.00–17.00 Mon–Sat (till 18.00 June–Aug),
11.00–17.00 Sun Ⓝ Bus: 10, 11, 11B, 13, 13A, 16, 16A, 19, 19A; DART: Connolly
Station. Admission charge

The James Joyce Centre

A centre dedicated to the life and works of James Joyce (who left
Dublin at an early age!). Here you can see the door to 7 Eccles Street,
where Leopold Bloom never lived, lots of first editions (banned for
most of the 20th century), photographs and more. For somewhere
with no Joyce connections at all except that a dancing master
mentioned in *Ulysses* once lived here, it's a fun place, full of
enthusiasts, and a good base for daily walking tours of the city,
including Leopold Bloom's route in *Ulysses* and an excellent tour
of Prospect Cemetery where Joyce's father is buried. Nice café
and bookshop. 🖈 35 North Great George's St 🕿 (01) 878 8547
Ⓦ www.jamesjoyce.ie 🕓 09.30–17.00 Mon–Sat Ⓝ Bus: 3, 10, 11,
11A, 13, 16A, 19, 19A, 22, 22A. Admission charge

RETAIL THERAPY

The streets around O'Connell Street form one of the shopping centres in the city. Three big indigenous department stores offer everything from electrical goods to hatpins, the Ilac shopping centre on Henry Street is full of little shops to explore, the Jervis Centre has a couple of big British stores and the streets leading off O'Connell – Talbot Street, Moore Street and Capel Street – all have something to offer, from daft Irish dancing kit to fake designer socks and antimacassars.

Arnotts A department store of the old school, tacked together from assorted buildings and full of things that your granny would buy as well as some modern clothes and a good coffee shop. ⓐ 12 Henry St ⓣ (01) 872 1111 ⓦ www.arnotts.ie ⓛ 09.00–18.30 Mon–Wed, Fri & Sat (open until 21.00 Thur), 12.00–18.00 Sun

◗ Clery's has a stately presence in the heart of Dublin

Clery's Purpose-built department store with huge windows and some stylish things inside, including some good craft items. ⓐ 18–27 O'Connell St ⓣ (01) 878 6000 ⓦ www.clerys.com ⓒ 09.00–18.00 Mon–Wed, Fri & Sat, 09.00–20.00 Sun

Dunnes The Irish answer to M&S, with respectable clothes and fashionable housewares. ⓐ Henry St ⓣ (01) 814 6224 ⓦ www.dunnesstores.ie ⓒ 09.00–19.00 Mon–Sat, 11.00–19.00 Sun

Easons Excellent bookstore and newsagent with an extensive selection of maps, walking books and local history. ⓐ 40 O'Connell St ⓣ (01) 858 3800 ⓦ www.eason.ie ⓒ 08.30–18.45 Mon–Sat, 12.45–17.45 Sun

⬤ *'Pound of cherries for a euro!'*

Moore Street Market Fruit and veg, Christmas wrapping paper, cheap toys, t-shirts and the like, all in a strong Dublin accent. ⏰ 07.00–15.30

Walton's Irish musical instruments as well as CDs and books. 📍 2 North Great George's St ☎ (01) 874 7805 ⏰ 09.00–18.00 Mon–Sat

TAKING A BREAK

North of the river falls a bit short in the taking-a-break stakes, but there are some good places to look out for if you need a getting-out-of-the-heaving-crowds-of-O'Connell-Street moment.

Beshoff £ ❶ Great no-nonsense fish and chip place. 📍 6 O'Connell St ⏰ 11.30–22.30 Mon–Sat

Café Royal £ ❷ Very popular, excellent-value carvery lunch. Nothing outrageous here, but some good, old-fashioned hotel food. Try the afternoon tea. 📍 Royal Dublin Hotel, O'Connell St ☎ (01) 873 3666 🌐 www.bestwestern.ie ⏰ 12.30–14.30 Mon–Fri

Epicurean Food Hall £ ❸ If you don't mind the hubbub this place is a seriously small food court with some esoteric stalls serving cuisine from around the world at very reasonable prices. 📍 Liffey St Lower ⏰ 11.30–18.30 Mon–Sat

Grand Central £ ❹ Nicely converted old bank building serving some good lunch options and good coffee. Come back in the evening for the bar scene. 📍 10–11 O'Connell St ☎ (01) 872 8658 ⏰ 11.00–23.30 Mon–Thur, 11.00–02.00 Fri & Sat, 12.30–23.00 Sun

Patrick Conway's £ ➎ Big open bar serving some good pub food all day until 20.00. ➋ 70 Parnell St ➊ (01) 873 2687 ⓦ www.patrickconways.com

Pravda £ ➏ Another café bar that really comes into its own in the evenings but is good for a wrap or a melt during the day. ➋ 35 Liffey St Lower ➊ (01) 874 0090 ➍ 12.00–23.30 Mon–Thur, 11.00–02.00 Fri & Sat, 12.30–23.00 Sun

◗ *The popular Pravda bar's peculiarity is its Russian features*

AFTER DARK

RESTAURANTS

101 Talbot ££ ❼ This warm and welcoming establishment has two particular points of recommendation: one, it's where the city's artistes eat, so you'll see some characters; two, it has stunning vegetarian options, and that's still rare in Dublin.
ⓐ 101 Talbot St ⓣ (01) 874 5011 ⓛ 17.00–23.00 Tues–Sat
ⓦ www.101talbot.com

Alilang Korean Restaurant ££ ❽ The city's only Korean restaurant, suitably adapted to the less fiery Irish palate. Here you can eat *kimchee*, barbecue your own food at the table and try the green tea and Korean beer. ❷ 102 Parnell St ❶ (01) 874 6766 ❷ 12.00–14.30, 17.30–23.30 Mon–Thur, 12.00–14.30, 17.30–00.30 Fri, 12.00–00.00 Sat & Sun

D One Restaurant ££–£££ ❾ One of the most strangely located restaurants in the city, this small but cutting edge glass box stands right on the banks of the Liffey. The cuisine is thoughtful, modern Irish. Very busy at lunchtime but there is a good-value early dinner menu till 19.30. Outdoor tables in summer. ❷ North Wall Quay ❶ (01) 856 1622 ❷ 12.00–15.00, 17.00–22.00 Mon–Sat, 12.00–17.00 Sun

Chapter One £££ ❿ One of the best restaurants in the city, this place has survived for many a year in the basement of the beautiful Dublin Writer's Museum. Excellent cooking, lots of organic food, and the theatre menu brings prices down to almost affordable. ❷ 18–19 Parnell Square ❶ (01) 873 2266 ❿ www.chapteronerestaurant.com ❷ 12.30–14.30, 18.00–23.00 Tues–Fri, 18.00–23.00 Sat

Halo £££ ⓫ Very stylish restaurant in the Morrison Hotel, and unusually for a hotel restaurant it serves excellent avant-garde food. Very young, wealthy clientele enjoy a seriously designed dining room. ❷ Morrison Hotel, Ormond Quay Lower ❶ (01) 887 2400 ❷ 19.00–22.30; Snack food is served in the bar 12.00–22.00 ❶ Reservations essential

CLUBS
The Academy A theatre, comedy and music venue with a club night on Saturdays, for which there's an entrance fee. Catch shows, stand-up and bands in concert in one of the many spaces.

ⓐ 57 Abbey St Middle ⓣ (01) 877 9999 ⓦ www.theacademydublin.com
ⓒ 22.00–03.00 Thur–Sat. Admission charge on Sat

Murphy's Laughter Lounge This stand-up comedy venue has it all – comfortable auditorium, cameras carrying the performances to two bars via enormous plasma screens, and some big names in comedy three nights a week. ⓐ 4–8 Eden Quay ⓣ (01) 878 3003 ⓒ 19.30 Thur–Sat. Admission charge

⬥ 'The Hags with the Bags' – no, seriously!

West of the city centre

The area west of the city centre is dominated by the enormous Phoenix Park (see page 103), the biggest public park in Europe, and behind it the Prospect Cemetery (see page 106) whose tombstones read like a roll-call of the public personalities of the last 150 years. Along the north bank of the Liffey is the newly renovated north quays area, which leads to Smithfield and then on to the Collins Barracks (see page 106) and the park. On the south side of the river are the Guinness Storehouse (see below) and Kilmainham Gaol (see page 105). A few other places are well worth seeking out a little way north and south of the river. It is while discovering this part of the city that you may find the Luas tram useful. There isn't much as yet in this area in the way of shops but one or two places are emerging.

SIGHTS & ATTRACTIONS

Dublin Zoo
A thoughtful zoo with its inmates as happy as such creatures can be. There is a train ride, wildlife shows, and several endangered species represented here. ❸ Phoenix Park ❶ (01) 474 8900 ⓦ www.dublinzoo.ie ⓛ 09.30–18.00 Mon–Sat, 10.30–18.00 Sun, Mar–Sept; 09.30–dusk Mon–Sat, 10.30–dusk Sun, Oct–Feb ⓝ Bus: 10, 10A (from O'Connell St), 25, 25A, 26, 66, 66A, 66B, 67, 67A (from Abbey St Middle), 68, 69. Admission charge

Guinness Storehouse
Its lack of high buildings and position in a valley surrounded by mountains makes Dublin a grand spot for getting up high and checking out the view. Besides offering a tour of the history of one

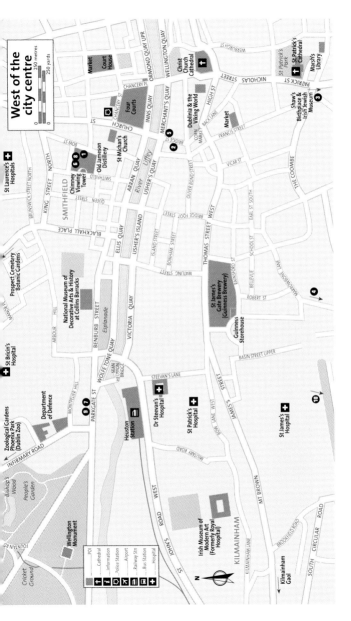

of the most famous breweries in the world, the Guinness Storehouse affords visitors the best opportunity for seeing the city from Gravity, the 360-degree viewing room at the top of the brewery. ➋ St James's Gate ☎ (01) 408 4800 ⓦ www.guinness-storehouse.com ⏲ 09.30–17.00 (till 20.00 July & Aug) ⓝ Bus: 51B, 78A (from Aston Quay), 123 (from O'Connell St); Luas: Red Line to St James's Hospital. Admission charge

Old Jameson Distillery

Another former glory of the city turned into a visitor centre. The Old Jameson Distillery visit is by tour around all the milling, mashing, fermenting tanks, ending up with a visit to the bar and a free whiskey-tasting session when the guide asks for a volunteer to taste several types of the tipple. Be ready! ➋ Bow St ☎ (01) 807 2355 ⓦ www.oldjamesondistillery.com ⏲ 09.30–18.00 (last tour begins at 17.30) ⓝ Bus: 68, 69, 79 (from Aston Quay), 90 (from Connolly & Heuston stations); Luas: Red Line to Smithfield. Admission charge

Phoenix Park

A whole day's visit in itself, this park is enormous, complete with its own herd of deer, a lacklustre visitor centre, a 17th-century tower house, a zoo, a police museum and lots of statuary. It is the home to the American ambassador and the Irish president, a war memorial garden designed by Lutyens and lots of people having a day out. Pick a sunny Saturday when there are free tours of Áras an Uachtaráin, the president's house. ☎ (01) 677 0095 ⓦ www.heritageireland.ie ⏲ Visitor centre 09.30– 17.30 (later in summer). Admission charge

◑ *Prepare yourself for an interesting tour*

CULTURE

Four Courts

This is Dublin culture at its most raw. The courts were built in the 18th century and still fulfil their original function. During court sittings you can go inside and watch criminals being found innocent or guilty. During the civil war these buildings were the site of a fierce battle between the two sides and, like the GPO, still bear the scars of battle.

ⓐ Inns Quay ⓒ Court sittings: 11.00–13.00 & 14.30–17.00 Oct–July

Irish Jewish Museum

In the 19th century, Dublin had a thriving Jewish quarter centred around the Portobello area of the city, with several synagogues, Jewish bakeries, craft workshops and shops. The area is fast becoming a bijou suburb for regular Dubliners and all that remains of the old culture is this little museum, set in what was once a small local synagogue. The upstairs remains the synagogue while downstairs a 19th-century Jewish kitchen is set out and there is an exhibition of memorabilia. This latter charts the Irish state's relationship with its resident Jewish community over the 20th century. ⓐ 3–4 Walworth St, off Victoria St ⓣ (01) 490 1857 ⓒ 11.00–15.30 Sun, Tues & Thur, May–Sept; 10.30–14.30 Sun, Oct–Apr ⓝ Bus: 16, 16A, 19, 19A, 122 (to Victoria St), 14, 14A, 15, 15A, 15B, 15C, 15X, 65, 65B, 83 (to South Richmond St)

Irish Museum of Modern Art

The museum hosts an ever-changing series of exhibitions of modern art from the national collection and foreign artists' work, set in the beautiful old Royal Hospital, one of the city's oldest buildings. The complex includes artists' studios which you can occasionally peek into, a formal garden, and Bully's Acre, a medieval burial ground. There are occasional tours of the building showing some of the surviving panelling and interiors. ⓐ Royal Hospital, Military Rd ⓣ (01) 612 9900 ⓦ www.imma.ie ⓛ 10.00–17.30 Tues–Sat, 12.00–17.30 Sun & bank holidays ⓑ Bus: 26 (from Wellington Quay), 51, 51B, 78, 79 (from Aston Quay), 90 (from Connolly & Tara stations), 123 (from O'Connell St)

Kilmainham Gaol

Opened in 1794 just in time to take in the rebels of the 1798 uprising and closing in 1924 after the last of the civil war prisoners were released, the gaol charts the history of the fight for Irish independence. The building was hated and stood derelict for decades after it was closed, until a few enthusiasts got permission to begin renovating it. Now that the pain of those early years has begun to wear off, the gaol has become a tourist attraction. Leading figures in Irish history spent time here, as did thieves, murderers and other criminals. Executions were carried out in the yard and the bodies of rebels buried in quicklime so that they couldn't be re-interred later. The visit is by tour and is a fascinating insight into what prison life was like. A small museum tells the history of the prison and can be visited before the tour begins. ⓐ Inchicore Rd, Kilmainham ⓣ (01) 453 5984 ⓦ www.heritageireland.ie ⓛ 09.30–18.00 Apr–Sept; 09.30–17.30 Mon–Sat, 10.00–18.00 Sun, Oct–Mar (last admission one hr before closing) ⓑ Bus: 51B, 51C, 78A, 79, 79A (from Aston Quay). Admission charge

Marsh's Library

The oldest public library in Ireland was built on the instructions of Bishop Marsh in 1701. The interior retains its original decoration and furnishings, with special cages around the most valuable books. In the visitors book you can see some famous names and in the Delmas Conservation Bindery you can watch old volumes being

restored. ❷ St Patrick's Close ☎ (01) 454 3511 🌐 www.marshlibrary.ie
🕐 10.00–13.00, 14.00–17.00 Mon & Wed–Fri, 10.00–13.00 Sat
🚍 Bus: 50, 54A, 56A (from Eden Quay). Admission charge

National Museum of Decorative Arts & History at Collins Barracks
This is one of those excellent museums that, instead of
concentrating on the preserved beautiful things that rich people
used, is filled with rustic furniture, half-reconstructed carriages,
everyday clothing, and more (as well, of course, as the regulation
expensive pots and ornaments of the wealthy). One section,
called the 'curators' choice', is a series of drawers which visitors
can open to observe the bits that the curators like the most.
There are videos on how to make straw baskets, courses for children,
a nice coffee shop and a bookshop. ❷ Benburb St ☎ (01) 677 7444
🌐 www.museum.ie 🕐 10.00–17.00 Tues–Sat, 14.00–17.00 Sun
🚍 Bus: 90 (from Aston Quay), 25, 25A, 66, 67 (from Abbey St Middle);
Luas: Red Line to Museum

Prospect Cemetery
Not normally associated with tourist destinations, this cemetery
is filled to the brim with the famous dead of Ireland. At the centre
is the enormous round tower dedicated to Parnell, one of the
country's major heroes. Here, too, is Michael Collins, buried close
to his sweetheart Kitty Kiernan. Enormous marble tombs mark
the dead of the Catholic hierarchy while more modest stones mark
Gerard Manley Hopkins and Brendan Behan (the circular hole in his
tombstone is often filled by his followers with a glass of Guinness).
The rebels of 1916 are for the most part here, as is De Valera, the

▶ *St Patrick: window by Heaton, Butler & Bayne (1890)*

country's first president, whose grave is the most vandalised one in the cemetery. Buy a map in the flower shop and wander, or join one of the excellent and amusing free tours. **ⓐ** Finglas Rd, Glasnevin **ⓘ** (01) 830 1133 **ⓦ** www.glasnevin-cemetery.ie **ⓛ** Dawn–dusk; Tours 14.30 Wed & Fri

St Michan's Church
Not yet turned into a heritage centre, this ancient church has much to offer visitors. It was founded in 1095 and was once the major church in this part of the city. The current building dates back to 1686. Its chief draw, however, is not in its architecture but in the vaults where the bodies of those interred have remained undecayed for several centuries. **ⓐ** Church St **ⓘ** (01) 872 4154 **ⓔ** stmichans@iol.ie **ⓛ** 10.00–12.30, 14.00–16.30 Mon–Fri, 14.00–16.30 Sat **ⓝ** Bus: 25, 25A, 26, 37, 51, 66, 66A, 68, 69, 134. Admission charge

St Patrick's Cathedral
Founded in 1191 this cathedral is built on a spot where St Patrick is said to have baptised the first Christians in Ireland. Much of the medieval interior of the church remains, although like Christ Church

CHANCING YOUR ARM
In the north transept of St Patrick's Cathedral is a wooden door, said to be 15th century. The hole in the door was made when, after a fight between two warring lords, one barricaded himself behind it in what was then the chapter house. The other, braver, lord cut the hole and stuck his arm through in an effort to make peace, giving us the expression 'chancing your arm'.

Cathedral, it had a 19th-century facelift. The tombs of Jonathan Swift and his companion Stella are here, as is an enormous monument to the Boyle family. As you enter the church, note the number of steps you have to go down to get in; the floor of the church was at street level in medieval times. ➌ St Patrick's Close, off Patrick Street ➊ (01) 475 4817 Ⓦ www.stpatrickscathedral.ie ⏰ 09.00–18.00 Mon–Fri, 09.00–17.00 Sat, 09.00–15.00 Sun Ⓑ Bus: 54A, 56A (from Eden Quay)

🔺 St Patrick's Cathedral choir was founded in 1432

Shaw's Birthplace

If you are fed up with Georgian Dublin then this is the place to visit, full of Victoriana and laid out just as a middle-class Victorian family would have lived. For a brief period, the family in question was that of George Bernard Shaw, although the Victorian theme is slightly more interesting than the literary one. ❷ 33 Synge St ❶ (01) 475 0854 Ⓦ www.visitdublin.com 🕒 10.00–13.00, 14.00–17.00 Mon & Tues, Thur & Fri, 14.00–17.00 Sat & Sun, May–Sept Ⓝ Bus: 16, 16A, 19, 19A, 122. Admission charge

RETAIL THERAPY

Out of the city centre, shops generally tend to be pretty functional places but there are a few streets worth a browse here. Francis Street contains a series of antique shops and markets dealing in bric-à-brac, furniture and memorabilia and is well worth seeking out. At Smithfield is Duck Lane, a tourist-dedicated place selling arts and crafts and housewares. The National Museum of Decorative Arts & History at Collins Barracks (see page 106) has a good bookshop, selling books on Irish history and some craft items, while at the Old Jameson Distillery (see page 103) there are whiskey-related things to buy.

TAKING A BREAK

1780 £ ❶ This public bar in the Old Jameson Distillery does a popular pub lunch. ❷ Bow St, Smithfield ❶ (01) 807 2355 🕒 12.00–14.30

The Brazen Head £ ❷ Better known for its nightly traditional music, this, the oldest pub in the city, also does a good carvery lunch and bar food. It also has an attractive restaurant upstairs serving

modern Irish cuisine in an olde worlde atmosphere. ⓐ 20 Bridge St
ⓣ (01) 677 9549 ⓦ www.brazenhead.com ⓛ 12.00–23.30

Jo'Burger £ ❸ No fewer than 140 different types of burger are available
here and, boy, are they big! Funky and fabulous. ⓐ 137 Rathmines Rd
ⓣ (01) 491 3731 ⓦ www.joburger.ie ⓛ 12.00–14.30

Lennox Café & Bistro £ ❹ Intimate and nicely decorated in an
olde-worlde style, the grub is great, the service greater. ⓐ 31 Lennox St
ⓣ (01) 478 9966 ⓛ 08.00–17.00 Mon–Fri, 09.30–17.00 Sat & Sun

O'Shea's Merchant £ ❺ Functional-looking bar that does a good
lunch. ⓐ 12 Bridge St Lower ⓣ (01) 679 3797 ⓛ Lunch 12.00–18.00

The Park Café Bar £ ❻ This extension of the lobby of the Park Inn does
filled rolls, panini, wraps and more substantial dishes. ⓐ Park Inn,
Smithfield ⓣ (01) 817 3838 ⓛ 12.00–14.30, 15.00–21.00

Nancy Hands ££–£££ ❼ Looks as if it's been there since the Industrial
Revolution. Carvery lunch, coffees and a pleasant place for a nibble.
ⓐ 30 Parkgate St ⓣ (01) 677 0177 ⓦ www.nancyhands.ie ⓛ 13.00–23.30

AFTER DARK

RESTAURANTS

Kelly & Ping ££ ❽ Asian fusion place serving an innovative mix
of Irish and Asian dishes. Quite stunning black and red décor; good
place to make a night of it before seeking out some late-night live
music. ⓐ Park Inn, Smithfield ⓣ (01) 814 8583 ⓛ 12.00–late Mon–Fri,
17.00–late Sat

● *Enjoy a drink and views of the city at the Gravity Bar (see page 103)*

Ryan's ££ ❾ Upstairs in this Victorian pub is a restaurant serving Irish cuisine in Victorian-style surroundings (see page 114).

Nonna Valentina ££–£££ ❿ Excellent Italian food, wonderful ambience and the service is perfect. Go on, argue with that.
ⓐ 1 Portobello Rd ① (01) 454 9866 ⓒ 12.00–22.30

BARS & CLUBS
The Brazen Head Live traditional music every night (see page 110).

The Chancery Inn Quaint and curious old pub which opens at 07.00 every morning except Sunday, serving traders from the nearby

Smithfield fruit and vegetable market. Colourful locals, and karaoke every Friday and Saturday night at 21.00. ② 1 Inns Quay ① (01) 677 0420 ⏰ 07.00–23.30 Mon–Thur, 07.00–late Fri & Sat

Cobblestone Cracking old pub which survived the devastation of rebranding Smithfield as a tourist attraction. Live traditional music downstairs and a pay-as-you-enter live venue upstairs. ② King St North ① (01) 872 1799 ⏰ 11.00–23.30

Dice Bar Hip, New York-style bar which has resisted the temptation to get themed. Occasional live music. Check listings for what's on. Nice cocktails. ② 79 Queen St, Smithfield ① (01) 633 3936 ⏰ 12.30–23.30 (later at weekends)

The Legal Eagle Occasionally known as 'The Bar', this place has DJs most nights and the occasional live music session. ⓐ 1–2 Chancery Place, Four Courts ⓘ (01) 873 5031 ⓒ 12.30–23.30 (later at weekends)

O'Shea's Merchant Set dancing most evenings upstairs after the food has been cleared away (see page 111).

Ryan's This place looks so good it has to be fake, but unlike Nancy Hands next door (see page 111), it's as real as they come. Lovely old bar fittings and a Victoriana restaurant upstairs. ⓐ 22 Parkgate St ⓘ (01) 677 6097 ⓒ 12.30–23.30 (later at weekends)

▶ *The outstanding beauty of Howth*

The northern coastline & Newgrange

For decades wealthy Dubliners have been leaving the city and heading for the towns to the north, commuting in each day and creating a suburban feel in these small places. If you want to venture out of Dublin, a trip north starts at Howth, which retains a sleepy, fishing-village demeanour. Beyond Howth, Malahide has lots to offer with a lovely coastal walk, Malahide Castle (see page 121) and gardens. Further north again, Skerries has some pretty coastline and a seaside-haven feel and is well worth considering as a place to stay outside the city. The highlight of a trip north, and one which is best conducted through a tour agency, is the trip to Newgrange in the Boyne Valley (see page 125), a 4,500-year-old, perfectly engineered underground series of passage tombs and burial chambers.

GETTING THERE

A railway line trundles its way north along the coast and all the seaside towns are easily accessed with the DART. For Newgrange there is a bus service from Busáras in Store Street directly to the Brú na Bóinne Visitor Centre, from where a shuttle bus takes you to the sites.

If you want to drive, the N1, then the M1 roads will take you out of the city. Otherwise, the areas and places in the chapter are well served by public transport, which is given under the following listings.

HOWTH

SIGHTS & ATTRACTIONS
Howth cliff walk
Howth is a pretty seaside town. A couple of wacky museums are

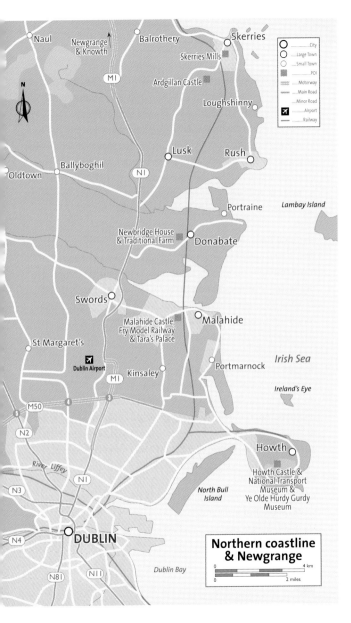

Northern coastline & Newgrange

located here and there are some interesting places to eat. The highlight of a day in Howth is the cliff walk around the Howth peninsula. Make your way across the grounds of Howth Castle to Carrickbrack Road, where a sign indicates the start of the cliff walk. An alternative is to start from Sutton Station where Station Road and then Greenfield Road will lead to the cliff walk. The paths are clearly marked and the walk takes about two hours, finishing in Balscadden Road in the village where there are lots of places to recuperate.

National Transport Museum

This is a bus-and-fire-engine fetishist's paradise, with 60 or more commercial vehicles dating back to the earliest forms of motorised transport. ⓐ Howth Castle Demesne ⓣ (01) 848 0831 ⓦ www.nationaltransportmuseum.org ⓛ 10.00–17.00 Mon–Sat, June–Aug; 14.00–17.00 Sat & Sun, Sept–May ⓝ Bus: 31, 31B (from Eden Quay); DART: Howth. Admission charge

Ye Olde Hurdy Gurdy Museum

Every bit as tacky as the name suggests. Old radios and TVs, Morse Code equipment, gramophones, etc. Worth visiting for some as a trip down memory lane. ⓐ Martello Tower, Abbey St ⓣ 086 815 4189 ⓛ 11.00–16.00 May–Oct; 11.00–16.00 Sat & Sun, Nov–Apr ⓝ Bus: 31, 31B (from Eden Quay); DART: Howth. Admission charge

TAKING A BREAK

Caffè Caira £ Seriously popular fish and chip shop with a few seats inside (but most people sit out on the harbour wall). No newspaper wrappers, but almost the real thing. ⓐ 1 East Pier ⓛ 12.30–21.00

The Bloody Stream ££ Café bar beside the station with a substantial lunch menu weekdays from 12.00 to 20.00 (till 18.30 weekends). The restaurant upstairs operates at weekends. Standard, well-cooked fare of steaks and salads, wraps and filled rolls. ❸ Howth Railway Station ❶ (01) 839 5076

AFTER DARK

Abbey Tavern ££ An 800-year-old tavern serving sound grub. Live music and Irish dancing after dinner in the evening. ❸ Abbey St ❶ (01) 839 0307 Ⓦ www.abbeytavern.ie Ⓛ 10.30–23.30, Show nightly in summer 20.45–22.30

🔺 *Choose a fish supper from a local vendor*

El Paso ££ Big Tex-Mex place with covered outdoor seating area and lots of spicy Mexican favourites. ⓐ 10 Harbour Rd ⓣ (01) 832 3334 ⓣ 18.30–23.00

Aqua ££–£££ Former exclusive yacht club now open to anyone with some plastic to flash. Lovely location with views over the harbour. Fresh seafood and some meat dishes. Excellent value early-bird menu from 17.30. ⓐ 1 West Pier ⓣ (01) 832 0690 ⓣ 13.00–16.00, 17.30–02.30 Tues–Sun

King Sitric £££ Long-established seafood restaurant with good sea views. Some very fresh and esoteric fish fill the menu. ⓐ East Pier ⓣ (01) 832 5235 ⓦ www.kingsitric.ie ⓣ 12.00–15.00, 19.30–22.30 Mon–Sat

ACCOMMODATION
Marine Hotel £–££ A little out of the way of Howth village but with lots of facilities that make up for it, and it's just a hop away from the Sutton Cross DART station. Pool, sauna, carvery lunch, good hotel dinner. ⓐ Sutton Cross ⓣ (01) 839 0000 ⓦ www.marinehotel.ie

King Sitric ££ Small guesthouse and restaurant with an excellent reputation. All eight rooms have sea views. In the heart of Howth village. ⓐ East Pier ⓣ (01) 832 5235 ⓦ www.kingsitric.ie

MALAHIDE

SIGHTS & ATTRACTIONS
Fry Model Railway
One for small boys and anoraks, this collection was put together by

Cyril Fry, a railway engineer. ⓐ Malahide Castle Demesne ⓣ (01) 846 3779
ⓦ www.visitdublin.com ⓒ 10.00–13.00, 14.00–16.30 Mon & Tues, Thur
& Fri, 13.00–18.00 Sun, Apr–Sept. Admission charge

Malahide Castle

Originally built in the 12th century and owned by the Talbot family
for 800 years, this fortified house has been restored to its original
condition and is open to the public by tour. It's a fascinating tour,
omitting only the below-stairs section, and includes a peek into
a haunted side room, and collections of silhouettes and model
furniture. A considerable number of portraits on permanent
loan from the National Gallery (see page 66) are also kept here.
The castle grounds are extensive and include a little walled

🔺 *Malahide Castle*

garden and the ruins of a 14th-century abbey. ☎ (01) 846 2184
🌐 www.malahidecastle.com 🕐 10.00–17.00 Mon–Sat, 10.00–18.00
Sun, Apr–Sept; 10.00–17.00 Mon–Sat, 11.00–17.00 Sun, Oct–Mar.
Admission charge

Newbridge House & Traditional Farm

This place is worth the effort of getting there, even with its slightly
more problematic access. It's an 18th-century mansion once owned
by the archbishop of Dublin. The rooms that are open to the public
are furnished in the original style, but, more interestingly, the house's
original outbuildings are intact and have been brought back to their
former condition, including the dairy that provided the bishop's milk
and butter, one of his estate workers' cottages, a smithy and a workshop.
In the extensive grounds is a traditional farm complete with the
animals that the bishop's household would have kept. ➋ Newbridge
Demesne, Donabate ☎ (01) 843 6534 🌐 www.fingalcoco.ie 🕐 10.00–13.00,
14.00–17.00 Tues–Sat, 14.00–18.00 Sun, Apr–Sept; 14.00–17.00 Sat &
Sun, Oct–Mar 🚆 Suburban Rail: northbound from Connolly or Pearse
St Station to Donabate, then a 15-minute walk; Bus: 33B from Eden
Quay to Donabate. Admission charge

Tara's Palace

Begun in 1980 and still in the process of completion, this is
every Barbie owner's dream. Oil paintings adorn the palace walls,
and the place is filled with crystal glassware, perfect miniature
furniture, state and private rooms, plus Oscar Wilde's mother's
dolls' house and lots of dolls and antique toys. ➋ The Courtyard,
Malahide Castle Demesne ☎ (01) 846 3779 🕐 10.45–16.45 Mon–Fri,
11.30–17.30 Sat & Sun, Apr–Sept; 11.30–17.30 Sat & Sun, Oct–Mar.
Admission charge

RETAIL THERAPY

Malahide is about the best you will find if you are desperate to do some shopping north of Dublin city centre. It is small enough to get to know all the shops in about 20 minutes – a couple of bookshops, some sophisticated dress shops, and a couple of charity shops where the wealthy of Malahide take their cast-offs.

TAKING A BREAK

Lounge Bar, White Sands Hotel £ If you've done the bracing seaside walk from Malahide, this is a great place to stop for a break. Coffee at the bar or lunch is available seven days a week. ❷ White Sands Hotel, Coast Rd, Portmarnock ❶ (01) 846 0420 ❸ 12.30–15.00 Mon–Sat, 12.30–18.00 Sun

Cruzzo Restaurant ££–£££ Trendy place doing modern Irish cuisine, coffees and a clubby atmosphere at night. ❷ The Marina, Malahide ❶ (01) 845 0599 ❿ www.cruzzo.ie ❸ 12.30–14.30, 18.00–22.15 Tues–Sat, 12.30–15.00, 18.00–22.00 Sun

AFTER DARK

Restaurants

Jaipur ££ Part of a successful chain of good Indian restaurants with classic Indian dishes, serving dinner from 17.30 to 23.00 daily. ❷ St James's Terrace ❶ (01) 845 5455

The Mad Fish ££ Stylish modern setting for respectable modern cooking. ❷ White Sands Hotel, Portmarnock ❶ (01) 846 0420 ❸ 18.30–21.30 Tues–Sat

Bars & pubs

Duffy's You can catch some traditional music on Thursday nights after 21.00. ⓐ Main St ⓣ (01) 845 0735 ⓛ 10.30–00.00

Gibney's With live music on Sundays and a comedy club on the last Thursday in the month. ⓐ New St ⓣ (01) 845 0863 ⓛ 10.30–23.30

Smyth's Lounge Live music and a heck of a good time. ⓐ New St ⓣ (01) 845 0960 ⓛ 10.30–00.00

ACCOMMODATION

White Sands Hotel ££ A bit inaccessible, but this place has an amazing location with sweeping sea views and a well-run, cosy atmosphere. Live music in the bar. Very useful place if you are driving, or there is a bus into Malahide right outside the hotel. Good value for what you get. ⓐ Coast Rd, Portmarnock ⓣ (01) 866 6000 ⓦ www.whitesandshotel.ie

SKERRIES

SIGHTS & ATTRACTIONS

Ardgillan Castle

Built in 1738, this house was in private hands until 1982. It has been furnished in the style of the 19th century and its biggest attraction is the below-stairs part where the working conditions and utensils of the family servants are to be seen. In the upper storeys of the house there is an exhibition of the Down Survey, commissioned by Oliver Cromwell. The most spectacular part of the visit, though, is the grounds. The house is set on a hill and from the wooded gardens there are fine views all the way to the Mountains of Mourne. You

can also visit a heated Victorian glasshouse, complete with
lemon trees, and a walled garden. Somewhere in the grounds, too,
is the ice house, used to keep perishable food cool in the summer.
ⓐ Balbriggan ⓘ (01) 849 2212 ⓛ House 11.00–18.00 Tues–Sun,
Apr–Sept; 11.00–16.30 Tues–Sun, Oct–Mar, Park 10.00–dusk
ⓝ Bus: 33 from Eden Quay; Suburban Rail: Skerries, then
a 30-minute walk. Admission charge

Newgrange & Knowth

Discovered in 1699, this Neolithic passage grave consists of a 19-m
(62-ft) sloping passage leading to a central chamber with a corbelled
roof. Set into this is a light box which allows sunlight into the room
for about 17 minutes around the winter solstice. Don't even think
about going there for that experience, as places for a visit are booked
for decades to come, but the operators have fitted up a fake sunlight

ⓞ An aerial view of Newgrange Megalithic Passage Tomb

so you can imagine what it must be like. The interior is decorated with carved lozenge and zigzag patterns and a massive stone covered the entrance, presumably to be pulled aside each year at the winter solstice. In summer people come here in droves and there is often a long wait for access.

Close to Newgrange and rather less well known is a whole series of Knowth passage tombs, the largest being two of these tombs built back to back. The eastern passage is an enormous 40 m (130 ft) long, and its chamber is built in the shape of a cross. Sadly, though, while the interior has many more decorated stones than Newgrange, it is not possible to enter the graves. The bus tours from the visitor centre can be taken to either or both Neolithic sites. ❸ Brú na Bóinne Visitor Centre, Donore ❶ (041) 988 0300 ⓦ www.heritageireland.ie, www.knowth.com ❺ 09.00–19.00 June–mid-Sept; 09.00–18.30 May & end Sept; 09.30–17.30 Mar–Apr & Oct; 09.30–17.00 Nov–Feb (last admission 45 mins before closing) ❷ Bus: from Busáras, Store St, to Donore. Admission charge

Skerries Mills

Not just a heritage centre, these are working mills, dating back to the 16th century and once owned by an Augustinian monastery. As water and wind power gave way to electricity, the mills fell into disuse, but the bakery operated right up until the 1980s. Now fully restored, the mills comprise two windmills and a water mill. You can watch the flour being ground and have a go yourself and then fill up with bread and cakes in the café. There's also a nice craft shop. The complex operates as the local tourist office too. ❸ Skerries ❶ (01) 849 5208 ⓦ www.skerriesmills.org ❺ 10.30–17.30 Apr–Sept; 10.30–16.30 Oct–Mar, closed Good Friday & two weeks over Christmas ❷ Bus: 33 from Eden Quay; Suburban Rail: Skerries. Admission charge

TAKING A BREAK

Parachute Café £ Coffee shop in the village with a children's play area and seating outside. Breakfast till noon. 🅐 47–48 Thomas Hand St 🛈 (01) 849 2322 🕒 09.00–17.30 Mon–Sat, 10.00–17.30 Sun

AFTER DARK

Stoop Your Head £–££ Seaside restaurant doing some good seafood. 🅐 Harbour Rd 🛈 (01) 849 2085 🕒 12.00–14.30, 18.00–21.30

Red Bank ££–£££ Excellent seafood restaurant. Choose your food while snacking on lovely hors d'oeuvres and an aperitif. Great service in a fun atmosphere. 🅐 7 Church St 🛈 (01) 849 1005 🕒 12.00–23.30

Bars & pubs

The village has several places where you can catch some (mostly traditional) live music in the evenings. Pubs generally put up notices outside telling you what's on offer each week. A couple of good spots are:

Joe May's There is live traditional music on Tuesdays. 🅐 Harbour Rd 🛈 (01) 849 1241 🕒 11.00–00.30

Nealon's Has music mid-week, usually on Wednesdays 🅐 12 Church St 🛈 (01) 849 0061 🕒 12.00–00.00

ACCOMMODATION

Redbank House ££ Seriously worth considering as a place to stay, Skerries has the added advantage of this excellent guesthouse where breakfast is the highlight of the day. Lots of golfers use this as a base. 🅐 5–7 Church St 🛈 (01) 849 1005

South of the city

Like its northern counterpart, the south of the city has formed from a series of small, quiet villages into an urban string. House prices rise as you leave the city, and the sea views, access to marinas and rural atmosphere explain why. Wandering around the streets and bars of Dalkey or Killiney you may well stumble upon the occasional Irish celeb, many of whom have settled in the area. Despite the urban sprawl, there is still much to see, most of it dominated by the overpowering and often grey outlines of Dublin Bay. Sights are listed according to the order in which you will approach them by the train travelling south.

GETTING THERE

The familiar and clunky DART will take you to your destination, offering unreal seascapes out of a commuter transport system window.

SIGHTS & ATTRACTIONS

Booterstown

When the train stops at Booterstown, from your DART window (or if you have a mind, jump off the train and look, but do wait until it stops) you can see a tiny wildlife sanctuary right beside the station. The little marsh here is home to some interesting sea and marsh bird life, which doesn't seem at all put off by the great green trains lumbering past every 20 minutes or so.

Dun Laoghaire

Rapidly becoming an urban centre in its own right, Dun Laoghaire was, before the advent of budget airlines, the first place that visitors

to Ireland encountered and, for those who bring their car over, it still is. With the ferry terminal close by and transport into the city so easy, this would make a good base for a stay in Dublin, particularly if the 24-hour life of the city begins to pall. Its grand Victorian houses and seafront are reminders of the time when it was a major holiday destination for Dubliners and its newer shopping centres and café bars reflect the consumer lifestyle of its present-day inhabitants. The Dun Laoghaire Piers, two piers which protect Dun Laoghaire harbour, are each over a mile long and both make a pleasant, if breezy, walk with views from the ends over Dublin Bay.

National Maritime Museum

One of those funky little museums put together by enthusiasts, containing a longboat captured from the French invaders of 1798, a large lens from the Bailey lighthouse at Howth and lots of model ships. It is set in the former Mariners' Church. ⓐ Haigh Terrace, Dun Laoghaire ⓘ (01) 280 0969 ⓛ 13.00–17.00 Apr–end Sept Ⓝ DART: Dun Laoghaire. Admission charge

Forty Foot

Named after the regiment which was once stationed here, the Forty Foot is a bathing place traditionally used only by men who wore no bathing clothes. You can still see the occasional nudist but now it is a mixed bathing area. ⓐ Sandycove Point Ⓝ Bus: 59 from Dun Laoghaire; DART: Sandycove

James Joyce Museum

James Joyce lived in this Martello tower for a week with his friend Oliver St John Gogarty and made it the scene of one of the opening pages of his novel *Ulysses*. Joyce fans will be able to re-create the scene and admire Joyce's guitar, some of his letters, and some rare first editions of his work. The tower is set out as it would have been when St John Gogarty lived there and you can go up to the roof for the views. ❸ Joyce Tower, Sandycove Point ❶ (01) 280 9265 ❤ www.visitdublin.com ⓛ 10.00–13.00, 14.00–17.00 Mon–Sat, 14.00–18.00 Sun, Apr–Sept ❷ Bus: 59 from Dun Laoghaire; DART: Sandycove. Admission charge

Dalkey Castle

Dublin's answer to Beverly Hills, Dalkey teems with ageing rock stars, celebrity chefs and actors waiting for that call to collect their Oscar. Besides the pretty coastal walks here, the main attraction is Dalkey Castle, one of six towers that once stood in the area and which were used to store goods brought into what was once Dublin's major harbour. Inside you can see the murder hole which defenders used to drop heavy objects down onto people they didn't like the look of, and other medieval features. The tower also serves as a heritage centre and guided walks of the area leave from here. ❸ Castle St, Dalkey ❶ (01) 285 8366 ❤ www.dalkeycastle.com ⓛ 09.30–17.00 Mon–Fri, Historical walks 11.45 Mon, 13.45 Wed, 11.45 Fri ❷ DART: Dalkey

Bray

Bray is a quiet, almost sleepy little Victorian seaside town which is filled with B&Bs and has a Victorian seafront complete with shingle beach. It is perfect for a day when the city just becomes too much and you need some space. The highlight of a trip to Bray is the 8-km (5-mile) cliff walk from Bray to Greystones. It is a bracing walk along clearly marked footpaths and the start can be found at the southern end of the promenade. From the village of Greystones it is possible

to catch bus 84 back to Bray. A shorter but more strenuous walk can be undertaken to the top of Bray Head from the same starting point. The path climbs to the top of the hill, offering stunning views over the Wicklow Mountains and all the way to Wales on a clear day. A less energetic option is a visit to the National Sea Life Centre, where you'll find 70 species of sea-living creatures, both local and otherwise, including shark, piranha, armour-plated starlet and more. Feeding times, talks and presentations are all on offer. **National Sea Life Centre** ⓐ Strand Road, Bray, Wicklow ① (01) 286 6939 ⓦ www.sealife.ie ⓛ 10.00–18.00 May–Sept; 11.00–17.00 Oct–Apr ⓝ DART: Bray. Admission charge

Enniskerry

Although it is only 19 km (12 miles) out of Dublin, you are definitely out of the city when you visit this bustling little market town at the foot of the Wicklow Mountains. The town owes its existence to the Wingfield family who laid out the original village in the 18th century. There are several interesting cafés which make this a good starting or finishing point for a walk in the hills, but the chief reason to visit is to see Powerscourt Gardens. The huge Powerscourt estate was created by the same Richard Wingfield who built the first rows of workers' cottages for his employees. At the heart of it is Powerscourt

SPIRIT-FILLED INSPIRATION

The story goes that the 19th-century designer of the Powerscourt Gardens, Daniel Robinson, was wheeled round the gardens in a wheelbarrow while he drank sherry to encourage his design skills to get to work.

House, built by Richard Castle in the first half of the 18th century. Sadly, the house was gutted by fire in 1974, just after it had been fully renovated, and restoration had to begin again and continues still. The real reason why hundreds of people make the visit here is to see the gardens, 20 hectares (49 acres) of parkland and formal gardens. The gardens were first laid out in the 18th century and then altered in the 19th. On entering the gardens you are given a map which highlights

△ *Powerscourt Gardens – imagine living here*

several different hour-long walks around the gardens, pointing out unusual and specimen plants. The sights include a Japanese garden, Italian garden, a pet cemetery, fountains and other statuary. A signposted walk of 6 km (4 miles) takes you to Powerscourt Waterfall, a 130-m (426-ft) fall of water, the highest in the British Isles and well worth the trek. ❷ Powerscourt Estate, Enniskerry ☎ (01) 204 6000 ⓦ www.powerscourt.ie ⏰ House and gardens 09.30–17.30 (shorter hours in winter), Waterfall 09.30–19.00 (summer); 10.30–dusk (winter) Ⓝ Bus: 44 from Hawkins St, Dublin. Admission charge

Russborough House

This is probably the finest extant house built in the Palladian style, with a great long string of curlicues and bits and pieces extending the front aspect of the house into an ornate wall far bigger than the house itself. It, like lots of the other houses in this style, was built in the mid-18th century, before the Act of Union put paid to the economic upsurgence of Ireland. Richard Castle built it for Joseph Leeson, or Lord Russborough, who, like many of his wealthy contemporaries, made his money from alcohol. In the 1950s the house passed into the hands of the people who owned the De Beers diamond mines and who brought to the house their art collection, most of which was later donated to the National Gallery. One of the chief reasons for coming here is to see the paintings from the collection which are displayed here – the exhibits change regularly. Visit is by tour, which takes in the important paintings. A second tour visits the bedrooms with their displays of silverware and furniture. ❷ 5 km (3 miles) southwest of Blessington ☎ (045) 865 239 ⓦ www.russborough.ie ⏰ 10.00–17.00 Ⓝ Bus: 65 from Eden Quay (90 minutes). Admission charge

THE WAY TO SEE THE COUNTRY

Here's what awaits you if you decide to take on the Wicklow Way – well, the first two days anyway:

Day 1: Join the route at Marlay Park in the south of Dublin (Bus: 47B). The walk travels south for 21 km (13 miles), is well signposted and well used by other walkers. The route passes through Kilmashogue Lane , through woods of the same name and up Two Rock Mountain to Glencullen, then across open moorland to Knockree, where there is a hostel, or you can make your way to Enniskerry (no bus service).

Day 2: The finest walk of all takes you past the Powerscourt Waterfall and then into the Wicklow Mountains with Sugarloaf and Maulin mountains as a backdrop. The route follows the Dargle River for a time and then reaches Lough Tay and carries on to Glendalough; a stiff walk of 29 km (18 miles). You can recuperate with hearty fare and a comfy bed at Glendalough.

The Wicklow Way

Wicklow is considered the garden of Dublin and some beautiful walks are possible through unspoiled countryside. The easiest way to experience hill-walking in the Wicklow Mountains is to follow part of the Wicklow Way, a signposted walking route of 211 km (131 miles). Although it is signposted it is important to carry a map of the route and a compass, as it's easy to get lost on the many crossing paths. East-West mapping produces a strip map, and OS Discovery series maps 50, 56 and 62 cover the whole of the route.

Glendalough

This is a series of medieval monastic sites set in some of Wicklow's most picturesque countryside. A trip here can involve little more than an hour-long guided tour around the sites or it can extend to a day's walk around the lakes or around Spink mountain using one of the guided walk books available from Easons (see page 94) or other bookshops. Set beside the R756, the Glendalough Visitor Centre offers an introduction to the two monastic sites, a small museum containing some of the stonework and a short audio-visual presentation on their history. The centre has leaflets describing what you will see and outlining one or two short walks around the lake. It is not necessary to pay the entrance fee to the visitor centre to go on to the lake or the ruins.

Two minutes away from the visitor centre is the first of the sites, the Lower Lake Monastic Sites, with the 10th-century round tower dominating the landscape and the ruins of the cathedral. The 12th-century priest's house was heavily restored in the 19th century. The most beautiful and intact building is St Kevin's Church, a two-storey oratory with a belfry. Also here is St Saviour's, a 12th-century Romanesque church with much of its decoration intact.

If all this medieval ruin hasn't been enough, you can walk on to the second set of ruins, the Upper Lake Monastic Sites. Here is Reefert Church, another Romanesque-style building, while a little further along is St Kevin's cell, a beehive hut, so called because it is built from corbelled slates, each one sitting a little above the other, forming a beehive shape. Monks would have come here to be alone and meditate. A path leads to a small waterfall and further on is St Kevin's Bed, a cave where the monk who founded this place is said to have spent some time. **Visitor Centre** ☎ 0404 45425 ⓦ www.wicklownationalpark.ie ⏰ 09.30–17.15 mid-Mar–Oct;

09.30–16.15 Nov–mid-Mar ⓥ Bus: St Kevin's Bus (ⓣ (01) 281 8119) departs daily from opposite the Mansion House in Dawson St, Dublin, at 11.30 & 18.00 Mon–Sat, 11.30 & 19.00 Sun; return services are 07.15 & 16.15 Mon–Fri, 09.45 & 17.40 Sat & Sun. Admission charge

🔺 The distinctive 'round tower' at Glendalough

RETAIL THERAPY

Avoca Handweavers Huge branch of the craft emporium set in a little site of its own, a 19th-century garden with some rare specimens of trees and plants. Rare, too, is the inexpensive café serving good food (see below). ⓐ Kilmacanogue, 4 km (2 ½ miles) south of Bray on N11 ⓣ (01) 286 7466 ⓛ 09.00–18.00 Mon–Fri, 09.30–18.00 Sat, Sun & bank holidays ⓝ Bus: 145 from Mountjoy Square, Dublin, or pick it up at Bray DART station

Blackrock Market Full of interesting clothes, bric-a-brac, antiques and handicrafts. ⓐ Blackrock, three stops before Dun Laoghaire on the DART ⓛ Sun

TAKING A BREAK

Avoca Handweavers £ Self-service restaurant with some excellent and original food. If you like it, buy the cookbook. ⓐ Kilmacanogue, South of Bray ⓣ (01) 286 7466 ⓛ 09.30–17.00 Mon–Fri, 10.00–17.00 Sat & Sun

Powerscourt Terrace Café £ In the remains of Powerscourt House, Enniskerry, this self-service place is another branch of Avoca and is worth seeking out. You don't have to pay the entrance fee for the gardens to find the café. ⓣ (01) 204 6070 or (01) 204 6000 ⓛ 09.30–17.30

Powerscourt Arms Hotel £–££ Bar food, and restaurant serving respectable hotel grub. ⓐ Main St, Enniskerry ⓣ (01) 282 8903 ⓛ 12.30–14.30, 18.00–21.00 Mon–Fri, 12.30–21.00 Sat & Sun

Seagreen £–££ Handy tea room for a dainty coffee or lunch. ❷ The Crescent, Monkstown ❶ (01) 202 0130 ❸ 09.00–18.00 Mon–Wed, 09.00–19.00 Thur & Fri, 09.00–18.30 Sat, 12.00–18.00 Sun

Mao Café Bar ££ Branch of the city centre cafeteria. No-nonsense, cafeteria-style Asian fusion with Malay, Thai, Chinese, Turkish and other influences. Seating outside. ❷ Pavilion Centre, Dun Laoghaire

⬤ *Take a seat at the Purple Ocean Restaurant*

(01) 214 8090 12.00–22.30 Mon–Thur, 12.00–23.00 Fri & Sat, 12.00–22.00 Sun

AFTER DARK

RESTAURANTS

Alexis ££ Fabulous bistro-style fare is on offer at this intimate little gem. 17–18 Patrick's Street, Dun Laoghaire (01) 280 8872 17.00–22.30

The Gastro Pub ££ Good value for family dining, and, unusually, the owners are happy for you to bring your own bottle. Marine Road, Dun Laoghaire (01) 214 5772 12.30– 22.00

The Queen's ££ A pub/restaurant complex with big-screen tellies and upstairs piano bar/restaurant. 12 Castle St, Dalkey (01) 285 4569 19.00–23.30

Purple Ocean Restaurant £££ Modern Irish seafood, harbour views and outdoor seating. St Michael's Pier, Dun Laoghaire (01) 284 5590 www.purpleocean.ie 19.30–23.00

ACCOMMODATION

Rochestown Lodge Hotel and Leisure Club ££ Facilities include pool spa, hydropool, steam room, fitness centre and sauna. Rochestown Av., Dun Laoghaire (01) 285 3555 www.rochestownlodge.com

▶ *Part of the giant Táin Bó Cuailgne mural in the Setanta Centre*

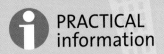

Directory

GETTING THERE

By air

Dublin airport has connections with 28 British airports and most airlines make their prices as competitive as they can, offering a few cheap seats on each flight and very cheap rates at off-peak times, and charging the earth at peak times. Book as far in advance as you can and try to travel off-peak. It can occasionally be cheaper to book two single flights rather than a return. Flight time from most British cities is about one hour. Airlines operating from UK:

Aer Arann ☎ 0800 5872324 🌐 www.aerarann.com
Aer Lingus ☎ 0845 084444 🌐 www.aerlingus.com
Air Wales ☎ 0870 7773131 🌐 www.airwales.co.uk
bmibaby ☎ 0870 2642229 🌐 www.bmibaby.com
British Airways ☎ 0870 8509850 🌐 www.britishairways.com
easyJet ☎ 0870 6000000 🌐 www.easyjet.com
Flybe ☎ 08705 676676 🌐 www.flybe.com
Flybmi ☎ 0870 6070555 🌐 www.flybmi.com
Ryanair ☎ 0871 2460000 🌐 www.ryanair.com

There are numerous connections between Dublin and most European countries with Ryanair, Aer Lingus, bmibaby and flybmi offering budget flights.

There are direct flights from seven US eastern cities to Dublin, mostly via Shannon. Flights from other cities cost considerably more and it often works out cheaper to fly to London Heathrow, Gatwick or Stansted and make a connection to one of the budget airlines. From Canada, Air Canada flies to Dublin via Heathrow from Montreal, Vancouver and Toronto. Again, check the price of a flight to London and a separate ticket from there to Ireland.

There are no direct flights to Dublin from Australia or New Zealand and you are best to check out flights to London and on to Dublin independently rather than use companies offering connections.

Many people are aware that air travel emits CO_2, which contributes to climate change. You may be interested in the possibility of lessening the environmental impact of your flight through the charity Climate Care, which offsets your CO_2 by funding environmental projects around the world. Visit Ⓦ www.climatecare.org

By rail
Ireland has a complex network of rail routes operated by **Iarnród Éireann** (Ⓦ www.irishrail.ie) connecting with Connolly Station or Heuston Station in Dublin (see page 49). Belfast trains connect with Connolly Station, while trains from cities in the south of Ireland

🔺 A convenient tram service runs through the city

connect with Heuston. Stena Line (see page 52) offers a train/ferry package from London to Dublin.

By road

Several coach companies operate a Dublin–London trip. This can be the cheapest means of transport but is certainly the slowest.
National Express Eurolines Runs regular daily services from London to Dublin via Birmingham (12 hours). ☎ 08705 143219 ⓦ www.eurolines.co.uk
Slattery's Has daily services from London, Bristol, Birmingham, Reading, Liverpool, Manchester and Leeds. ☎ 0800 515900 ⓦ www.slatterys.com

By water

There are two entry points into the city by ferry: Dun Laoghaire and Dublin Port in the city.
Irish Ferries Sail from Holyhead to Dublin Port (3 $\frac{1}{4}$ hours).
☎ 08705 171717 ⓦ www.irishferries.ie
Sea Cat Sail from Liverpool (4 hours) and the Isle of Man (2 $\frac{3}{4}$ hours).
☎ 08705 523523 ⓦ www.seacat.co.uk

ENTRY FORMALITIES

All visitors to Dublin from abroad need a valid passport except British nationals who do, however, need some form of photographic ID. EU citizens may stay in Dublin indefinitely without a visa. Visitors from the USA, Canada, Australia and New Zealand may stay for three months without a visa and this can be extended at Harcourt St Garda Síochána (Police Station).

For EU travellers there are no customs duties and no duty free restrictions, although you may have to show that the items you bring in are for personal use and not for resale. Travellers from outside the EU can bring in 200 cigarettes, 1 litre of spirits or 2 litres of wine, 60 ml of perfume and 250 ml of eau de toilette. Pets can travel from Britain and Northern Ireland without quarantine. Dogs and cats from the EU may be brought into the country if they have been fitted with a microchip, vaccinated against rabies and blood-tested six months before entry.

MONEY

Ireland is a member of the Eurozone. This has seven banknotes – €5, €10, €20, €50, €100, €200 and €500. Coins come in denominations of €1, €2 and 1, 2, 5, 10, 20 and 50 cents. There are 24-hour ATMs located outside most banks, in railway stations and at the airport, which will accept cards with Cirrus and Maestro symbols. You can also withdraw cash using VISA, Access and MasterCard. VISA and MasterCard are universally accepted, although you will need a pin number. American Express and Diners' Club cards are less widely used.

Traveller's cheques are a safe way of carrying money and can be changed at post offices and banks, although a commission will be charged. You will need some form of photographic identification. Changing cash can be an expensive business, especially in hotels. The best rates are at the banks but there are also bureaux de change, which operate outside banking hours. Visitors from outside the EU can obtain a refund of VAT on purchases if they leave within two months and if the shop their item was purchased from belongs to the Retail Export Scheme.

HEALTH, SAFETY & CRIME

No special health precautions are necessary before arriving in Ireland. Tap water is safe to drink. EU citizens are entitled to the same medical care as Irish citizens although you must bring a European Health

Insurance Card (EHIC) with you. The British website for ordering these cards is Ⓦ www.ehic.org.uk. (This replaces the old E111 form.) A visit to a GP in Ireland will entail a consultation fee, although any tests will be included in the price. A prescription charge will be levied for any medicines, around €15 for each item. These fees are not refundable. In Dublin a consultation will cost around €50. Visitors from both the UK and outside Europe should seriously consider medical insurance when visiting Ireland, although emergency medical treatment carries a fee of €50 , and there is usually a long wait except of course in life and death situations. Contraception is available over the counter in Ireland but the 'morning after' pill can be obtained only on prescription. In an emergency at weekends the **Family Planning Association** (Ⓔ 5/7 Cathal Brugha St Ⓣ (01) 872 7088) is open 09.00–16.00 Sat, 14.00–17.00 Sun Ⓘ All public buildings are smoke-free areas

Some handy websites that give health advice are:
American sites for travellers Ⓦ www.cdc.gov/travel, www.healthfinder.com
British government health and travel advice
Ⓦ www.doh.gov.uk/travellers, www.fco.gov.uk/travel
Travel Health Online Ⓦ www.travelhealth.co.uk
Useful tips and information Ⓦ www.tripprep.com
World Health Organisation Ⓦ www.who.int/en

Like all big cities, Dublin has its share of street crime. Personal belongings should be taken care of and kept out of sight. Carry a shoulder bag across the chest rather than hanging from a shoulder. Take care at ATMs in particular. Car break-ins are also commonplace. While it is safe to walk around most of the well-lit and busy city centre streets until late into the evening, things can get quite rowdy in the early hours at weekends in Temple Bar, O'Connell Street, Camden

Street, Grafton Street and Harcourt Street. Needless to say, Phoenix Park is not a safe place at night. Dublin also has its share of beggars who, for the most part, are model citizens compared with the drunken hen parties at 02.00. Many sell the *Big Issue* magazine and carry certification.

Hitchhiking was once common in Ireland, even in Dublin. It is still fairly safe in rural areas but is not recommended around Dublin, particularly if you are alone. Another hazard in Dublin is traffic. If it isn't gridlocked, it is travelling very quickly through the city streets and crossing roads can be hazardous. College Green, the junction in front of Trinity College, is particularly hazardous since speeding traffic travels from several different directions as the lights change and pedestrians get tired of waiting to cross safely. In other places there simply is no way to cross safely, and in others you can set off to cross when the green man flashes and halfway across the junction he's turned red.

The police force is called Garda Síochána; officers wear navy blue uniforms and travel in blue and white cars labelled Garda Síochána. Usually spoken of as guards, they generally do not carry guns. Pairs of pedestrian guards are an occasional sight around the main shopping streets and in Temple Bar. They become much more visible in the early hours, especially at weekends.

ⓘ Possession of even tiny amounts of cannabis is a crime in Ireland and will not be ignored.

OPENING HOURS

Shops are generally open 09.00 to 17.30 Monday to Saturday, with many of the city centre stores opening later and staying open until 20.00 on Thursdays, and open 13.00 to 17.00 on Sundays. Banking hours are usually 10.00 to 16.00 Monday to Friday. Some banks open late on Thursdays.

TOILETS

There are public toilets in all shopping centres and department stores, and toilets for customers' use in restaurants and bars. There is usually a small charge to use those in shopping centres and bartenders can occasionally get shirty if you just wander in and use the toilet. Toilets are marked by little men and women symbols on the doors but might occasionally be marked *fir* for men or *mná* for women.

CHILDREN

Dublin loves children and is a child-friendly city, apart from the traffic. Children are welcome in pubs during the day and restaurants often have child seats and menus or will serve half portions. There are lots of green spaces for playing in and amusing statuary all over the city to climb over. Even travelling on the DART is fun. Sights that are

● *Ha'penny Bridge and Liffey Voyage river cruise boat*

particularly suited to children include Dublinia (see page 78), where there are smells, things to poke and people dressed up in silly costumes. For more silliness, try the **Viking Splash Tour** (❶ (01) 707 6000 ⓦ www.vikingsplash.ie). This is an amphibious vehicle, decorated to look like a longboat, which tours the Viking sites of the city and then drives into the Grand Canal Harbour. The pick-up point is beside St Patrick's Cathedral or St Stephen's Green. More watery fun can be had on the **Liffey Voyage** (❶ (01) 473 4082 ⓦ www.liffeyvoyage.ie), a river trip which departs from a landing station off the boardwalk at Bachelors Walk. Kiddies love animals, of course, so a trip to Dublin Zoo (see page 100) might entertain restive minds. Meanwhile the National Sea Life Centre at Bray (see page 132), has a petting zoo, train rides, a beach and a hill to climb. All parents will know that behind the most angelic of smiles lurks a trainee psychopath, and little ones with a taste for the macabre will be fascinated by the mummified bodies at St Michan's Church (see page 108).

COMMUNICATIONS

Internet

Most hotels and hostels have internet access for guests and there are internet cafés located around the city. Try:

Global Internet Café 🔘 8 O'Connell St Lower 🔘 (01) 878 0295

TELEPHONING THE REPUBLIC OF IRELAND

Dublin phone numbers have seven digits. If you are calling from outside the city you must add the area code (01). To call from abroad, dial the international code first (usually 00), then the country code (353), the area code minus the initial 0, and the local number.

TELEPHONING ABROAD

To phone abroad, dial 00 first, then the country code, followed by the area code (minus the initial 0 if there is one) and the local number. Country codes:

Australia 61	New Zealand 64
Canada 1	South Africa 27
France 33	UK 44
Germany 49	USA 1

National directory (Ireland and Northern Ireland) 🔘 11811 or 11818
International directory (including UK) 🔘 11850 or 11860

Phone

Public phones in Ireland take both credit cards and coins. You can also buy pre-paid phonecards from newsagents and 24-hour grocery stores. Avoid using the phone in your hotel bedroom; hotel rates can be very high.

Your mobile phone should work in Ireland if you have instructed your provider to turn on the 'roaming' option. Before you use it, check how much it will cost to use. Companies often charge for receiving texts and phone calls as well as making calls from abroad.

Post

The main GPO is in O'Connell Street. There are sub-post offices in Parnell Street, Aston Place, Earlsfort Terrace, Merrion Row, Parkgate Street, Usher's Quay, Ormond Quay Upper and Andrew Street (🕐 09.00–17.30 Mon–Fri, 09.00–13.00 Sat). A 50-g letter to a destination in Ireland or Northern Ireland is €0.48 and the same letter to Britain or the rest of the world costs €0.75. See 🌐 www.anpost.ie
O'Connell Street GPO 📞 (01) 705 7000 🕐 08.00–20.00 Mon–Sat, 10.00–18.30 Sun & bank holidays

ELECTRICITY

The electricity supply is 220–240 volts, 50 Hertz. Plugs have three square pins as in the UK. Adapters for US and European appliances can be bought at the airport, from electrical shops around the city or from Dublin Tourism (see page 152).

TRAVELLERS WITH DISABILITIES

All newer buildings and public transport have wheelchair access and most hotels have disability-friendly rooms. For individual bus routes contact Dublin Bus. DART and Iarnród Éireann are less

PRACTICAL INFORMATION

disabled-friendly simply because they are older, although ramps can
be provided with prior notice. Restaurants must provide accessible
toilet facilities. Some of the city's sights may be inaccessible to
wheelchair users. For more information, contact the following:

Dublin Bus Customer Service 🅐 59 O'Connell St 🅣 (01) 873 4222
🅦 www.dublinbus.ie

Iarnród Éireann Offers the free booklet *Guide for Mobility-impaired
Passengers.* 🅣 (01) 703 2369

Irish Wheelchair Association 🅣 (01) 818 6400 🅦 www.iwa.ie

National Disability Authority 🅣 (01) 608 0400 🅦 www.nda.ie

Restaurants Association of Ireland Provides the free booklet *Dining
in Ireland.* 🅣 (01) 677 9901

TOURIST INFORMATION

Tourist offices

Dublin Tourism A walk-in service (no telephone) that includes
accommodation advice and bookings, ferry, sport and concert tickets,
a car-hire desk, free leaflets and an extensive book and map shop.
🅐 St Andrew's Church, Suffolk St

Other offices around the city are at the following:

Arrivals Hall Dublin Airport Accommodation advice and booking, ferry,
sport and concert tickets and general information. 🅞 08.00–22.00

Dun Laoghaire Ferry Terminal 🅞 10.00–18.00 Mon–Sat

Fáilte Ireland 🅐 Baggot St Bridge 🅞 09.30–12.00, 12.30–17.00

Temple Bar Information Centre For information about what's on
in Temple Bar. 🅐 12 Essex St East 🅦 www.visit-templebar.com

Tourist websites

General 🅦 www.tourismireland.com

Australia 🅦 www.tourismireland.com.au

France Ⓦ www.irlande-tourisme.fr
Germany Ⓦ www.irishtouristboard.de
USA Ⓦ www.shamrock.org

BACKGROUND READING

Dublin by Joss Lynam. Suggests 35 walks in the Dublin region.
Dublin: A Celebration by Pat Liddy. Too big for your suitcase but check it out in the national library for the low-down on all the major buildings and statuary.
The Complete Wicklow Way by J B Malone. A guide to the long-distance walk.
The Irish Heritage Cookbook by Margaret Johnson. Try out some of the dishes you've enjoyed in Dublin.
The Rising by B Tóibin. Love story set in the days leading up to the Easter Rising 1916.
The Speckled People by Hugo Hamilton. Biographical account of a boy growing up in Dublin.
The Truth About the Irish by Terry Eagleton. Everything you wanted to know but were afraid to ask.

Emergencies

The following are emergency free-call numbers:

Ambulance ❶ 999
Fire ❶ 999
Police ❶ 999

MEDICAL SERVICES

In a medical emergency call ❶ 999 for an ambulance. If your condition is not so serious, you can contact the **Eastern Region Health Authority** (❶ (01) 620 1600), which has a list of doctors. Your hotel will also be able to supply a contact for a GP. Out of surgery hours you can go to one of the A&E departments of the city's hospitals, where you can have a long wait unless it is a life-or-death situation. The best is at **Mater Misericordiae Hospital** (❷ Eccles St ❶ (01) 830 2000).

In a dental emergency during working hours, go to the **Dental Hospital** (❷ Lincoln Place ❶ (01) 612 7200 ❸ 09.00–17.00). Between 17.00 and 23.00, phone the hospital and you will be contacted within two hours by a dentist. After 23.00 you must go to a regular A&E (see above).

POLICE

There are police stations (identified by a blue lamp

○ *Garda is the name of the Irish Police*

above the door with 'Garda' written on it) in the following:

Fitzgibbon St ☎ (01) 666 8400

Harcourt Square ☎ (01) 666 6666

Pearse St ☎ (01) 666 9000

Store St ☎ (01) 666 8000

You should make a note before you travel of the number to ring in the event of a lost or stolen credit card. Any theft should be reported to **Tourism Victim Support** (🅰 Garda HQ, Harcourt Square ☎ (01) 478 5295). An incident report should be collected for insurance purposes.

EMBASSIES & CONSULATES

Australia 🅰 Fitzwilliam House, Wilton Terrace ☎ (01) 664 5300, after-hours emergency freephone to Canberra 1800 556 197 🕒 08.30–16.30 Mon–Fri

New Zealand In an emergency contact the New Zealand embassy in London. ☎ 00 44 20 7930 8422 🌐 www.nzembassy.com/uk

South Africa 🅰 Alexandra House, Earlsfort Centre, Earlsfort Terrace ☎ (01) 660 4233, after-hours emergency phone 087 050 6934

UK For lost passports, you must wait till office hours or return to Britain without one (but get a police report). 🅰 31 Merrion Rd ☎ (01) 205 3700, after-hours emergency (arrest, serious accident) phone 086 243 4655 🕒 09.00–17.00 (passports & visas shorter opening hours)

USA 🅰 42 Elgin Rd ☎ (01) 668 8777, after-hours emergency phone ☎ (01) 668 9464 🌐 www.dublin.usembassy.gov

WHAT'S IN YOUR GUIDEBOOK?

Independent authors Impartial up-to-date information from our travel experts who meticulously source local knowledge.

Experience Thomas Cook's 165 years in the travel industry and guidebook publishing enriches every word with expertise you can trust.

Travel know-how Contributions by thousands of staff around the globe, each one living and breathing travel.

Editors Travel-publishing professionals, pulling everything together to craft a perfect blend of words, pictures, maps and design.

You, the traveller We deliver a practical, no-nonsense approach to information, geared to how you really use it.

Editorial/project management: Lisa Plumridge
Copy editor: Paul Hines
Layout/DTP: Alison Rayner
Proofreader: Wendy Janes

SPOTTED YOUR NEXT CITY BREAK?

...then these lightweight CitySpots pocket guides will have you in the know in no time, wherever you're heading. Covering over 80 cities worldwide, they're packed with detail on the most important urban attractions from shopping and sights to non-stop nightlife; knocking spots off chunkier, clunkier versions.

Aarhus	Geneva	Palermo
Amsterdam	Genoa	Palma
Antwerp	Glasgow	Paris
Athens	Gothenburg	Prague
Bangkok	Granada	Porto
Barcelona	Hamburg	Reykjavik
Belfast	Hanover	Riga
Belgrade	Helsinki	Rome
Berlin	Hong Kong	Rotterdam
Bilbao	Istanbul	Salzburg
Bologna	Kiev	Sarajevo
Bordeaux	Krakow	Seville
Bratislava	Kuala Lumpur	Singapore
Bruges	Leipzig	Sofia
Brussels	Lille	Stockholm
Bucharest	Lisbon	Strasbourg
Budapest	Ljubljana	St Petersburg
Cairo	London	Tallinn
Cape Town	Los Angeles	Tirana
Cardiff	Lyon	Tokyo
Cologne	Madrid	Toulouse
Copenhagen	Marrakech	Turin
Cork	Marseilles	Valencia
Dubai	Milan	Venice
Dublin	Monte Carlo	Verona
Dubrovnik	Moscow	Vienna
Düsseldorf	Munich	Vilnius
Edinburgh	Naples	Warsaw
Florence	New York	Zagreb
Frankfurt	Nice	Zurich
Gdansk	Oslo	

The publishers would like to thank the following individuals and organisations for supplying their copyright photographs for this book: Alamy Images, pages 19, 29 & 121; Paolo Bassetti, pages 63 & 65; dahon, page 21; dodger, pages 25 & 112–3; Dreamstime.com (Uwe Blosfeld, pages 40–1; Marek Slusarczyk, pages 148–9); Lyn Gateley, page 17; jaqian, page 85; Karen, page 49; Mark Zanzig (www.zanzig.com), pages 42 & 59; Mermaid Café, page 82; William Murphy, pages 10, 26 & 154; Pictures Colour Library, pages 5, 53, 57, 107, 115, 133 & 137; Robert Harding World Imagery, pages 13, 45 & 109; Phil Romans, page 38; Sento, page 23; Sherland Entertainments Ltd, page 69; TASCO www.visit-templebar.com, page 9; Ruben Zantingh-Bozic, pages 96–7; Ian Wilson, page 7; Pat Levy, all others.

Send your thoughts to
books@thomascook.com

- Found a great bar, club, shop or must-see sight that we don't feature?
- Like to tip us off about any information that needs a little updating?
- Want to tell us what you love about this handy little guidebook and more importantly how we can make it even handier?

Then here's your chance to tell all! Send us ideas, discoveries and recommendations today and then look out for your valuable input in the next edition of this title.

Email the above address (stating the title) or write to:
CitySpots Project Editor, Thomas Cook Publishing, PO Box 227, Coningsby Road, Peterborough PE3 8SB, UK.